Tales of

An Old "Border Town"

and

Along The Kankakee

Tales of
An Old "Border Town"

and

Along The Kankakee

A Collection of Historical Facts and Intimate
Personal Sketches of the Days of the Pioneers
in Momence, Illinois, and the Hunting
Grounds of the Kankakee Marsh and "Bogus
Island"

BURT E. BURROUGHS

Author of Legends and Tales of Homeland on the
Kankakee,
California Letters, Etc.

FOWLER, INDIANA
THE BENTON REVIEW SHOP

LORAIN BEEBE LYNDS
Kankakee County's First School Teacher and
Postmistress, Who Lived to the Great Age of
Ninety-Three

FOREWORD

When Burt Burroughs wrote this book almost sixty years ago, he realized that the pioneers and their stories were doomed to be forgotten very quickly unless there were to be a record made of their lives and times. We are grateful to him, for by writing "," Mr. Burroughs left the Momence community a legacy of great worth. His book lets us visualize those early days when the prairies and forests were peopled by the Indians; we can trace the movement of those hardy souls who came by covered wagon from the East and from Canada; we are intrigued by their adventures with the horse-thieves and counterfeiters. Because of Burt Burroughs' books we have come to know of our heritage.

During the years since the publication of this book in 1925, the numbers of copies have dwindled. Loss and theft have taken their toll. Those fortunate enough to own an original copy of the book have become loath to lend it to any would-be reader.

So, it is that in planning for the celebration of the Sesquicentennial anniversary of Momence in 1984 the committee has had this book reprinted in order that it may once more be read by everyone who has ever called Momence "home." It is for our children and grandchildren too, for it would be sad indeed for coming generations to miss the rich inheritance of anecdote and reminiscence which this book gives the reader.

It is appropriate, then, that the re-issue of this book be a signal part of the homage we pay to Momence, our beloved old town on the river, as it reaches its 150th birthday.

MOMENCE 1984 SESQUICENTENNIAL COMMITTEE

Copyrighted, 1925, BURT K. BURROUGHS Kankakee, Illinois.

Parts of this reprint were scanned from an original 1925 Edition which was signed by Burt Burroughs and is in the library of the University of Illinois.

Kevin McNulty, Sr. Publisher

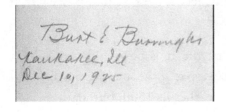

TALES OF AN
OLD BORDER TOWN
and Along the Kankakee

BY

BURT E. BURROUGHS

1925 "Red" Original Edition

FROM THE EDITOR

KMC Publishing Company is pleased to offer what is, "officially," the fourth printing of Burt E Boroughs' definitive work on the origins of Momence, Illinois.

"Tales of An Old "Border Town" and Along the Kankakee," was written in 1925 and printed locally. It was, of course, a hardcover book and had a red cover. Few are found today.

The book was reprinted in 1984 during the Momence Sesquicentennial Festival, headed by noted historian and author, Kathleen "Kay" Hess, making that release the 2nd printing. In that edition, photo quality was diminished due to the lack of technology we enjoy today. Demand for the '84 work resulted in a second release in 1985.

In addition to leading efforts to reprint the Burroughs book in '84, Kay Hess also compiled her weekly articles that appeared in the Momence Progress Reporter Newspaper leading up to the Sesquicentennial Celebration. The resulting "Momence...The making of a River Town," was a monumental work updating Burroughs, providing detailed accounts of family lineages, and gifting us with over 175 photographs rarely seen before.

KMC Publishing Company reprinted Kay Hess' book in 2013 with the permission of the family. It seems fitting, as we approach one-hundred years since Burroughs' work, to provide today's aficionados of Momence History with a new record of the great 1925 work.

As we did with Kay's book, we have utilized today's digital technology to improve the quality of all photos in this released.

We've been careful to maintain the original English language as it was used in 1925 by Burroughs but have updated some of the common uses of certain "two word" phrases that have now blended into one and also implemented or deleted some common hyphenated words in today's usage.

But in the main, we have left Burroughs alone. He deserves ultimate respect for his work and no editor should pretend to understand the intentions, uses of subtleties of the spoken word from one hundred years prior.

Burroughs's accounts of local language, his descriptions of the many characters of frontier Momence and his humorous descriptions of the town's ongoings, particularly those involving the local Pottawattamie Indians is precious. The reader will notice some variation in the spelling of some common words and, indeed, an occasional proper noun. Naturally, we have left these untouched.

I hope you enjoyed the first written account of Momence, Illinois in this new format. Momence is the first city in Northeastern Illinois and is an amazing profile of America's frontier and the settlement of the Illinois Territory.

Kevin McNulty, Sr
Publisher
August, 2018

PREFACE

To Noel Le Vasseur is accorded the honor of being the first white settler within the borders of Kankakee county as we know it today. He built his cabin of logs in the timber known as "LaPointe," or Bourbonnais, in the year 1832. In 1833, William Lacy built a log cabin on a ford of the Kankakee ten miles west of the Indiana state-line which was known later as "Upper Crossing," or Westport. A year later Asher Sargeant creaked up to the Kankakee with his ox-drawn wagon and built the first habitation on the present site of Momence, a mile west of where Lacy settled. These three settlements of 1832, 1833 and 1834, just one year apart, have had variously checkered careers. In the end, however, Momence outstripped them all. "Upper Crossing," today, is but a memory. It has faded completely from the face of the earth. Not so with Bourbonnais. It is a bright, clean, contented little village that neither gains nor loses appreciably but is content to hold its own in these days of turmoil and strife.

Momence of the old border days was a regular he- man's town. Situated on the river and on the edge of that vast marsh paradise of nearby Indiana, it was for years a sort of capital for the country roundabout, the focal point towards which the thoughts and steps of the wilderness population often turned. Here supplies of powder and shot were to be had and here, also, a fellow with a "thirst" could deluge the inner man to his heart's content with no one to say him nay, so long as he had a raccoon or mink pelt left to pay for it. If, in the full and complete enjoyment of his debauch, he elected to stow himself in a corner on the puncheon floor and sleep it off, that was his business. If he chose to run amuck that, also, was his privilege. There were no "stop and go" signs, no village marshal looming behind a "tin" star, no law except the law of force. It was the day of the "border."

Writing of these things in this day is no easy task. We realize with regret that it was undertaken too late to do full justice to the life story of a border settlement that has, after many vicissitudes, emerged into a well-ordered city. Her pioneers sleep today hard by the scene of their former endeavors, but their voices are stilled. They left no written records, in the main, and of the things they said and the things they did we collect but fragments in this day and count ourselves fortunate. In this volume we have incorporated historical fact together with legend, incident, and story of the old days which are likely to prove most valuable, in their narrative setting, to the reading public. The reader is forewarned that this little volume is not designed as, a compendium of local history, exactly. Rather would we have it remembered for its narratives of a day and its people long since passed on—a day when the middle western empire (which included the beautiful valley of the Kankakee) was in the making—an empire peopled by "homespun" giants, who deserve, at least, as a reward of having lived, the poor boon of remembrance.

BURT E. BURROUGHS
Kankakee Illinois
September 1, 1925.

APPRECIATIONS

Were it not that people, in the main, are friendly, kindly, responsive in a marked degree to the importunities of the seeker after stories and facts of the great Pioneer Age, of the Kankakee Valley, a volume such as this would be **well-nigh** impossible. I have learned something of the friendly quality of Kankakee county folk in the last two years and a half and, let me add, this also applies to those portions of Newton and Lake counties in Indiana, wherein is located the basin of the Kankakee which we know as the "Kankakee Marsh" and "Beaver Lake." From the humblest dweller of the marsh on up through the varying human strata wherein is represented the busy man and the idler, the man of affluence and the man of small affairs—all have listened to the appeal for some fact of interest concerning the old days of our fathers and mothers and responded as they' were able, willingly and gladly. If this volume should be found to contain data and incidents out of the ordinary, it is attributable. in large part, to that spirit on the part of the people Which seeks to be obliging.

Mr. C. M. C. Buntain, of Kankakee, has permitted me to use sketches of the late W. W. Parish and the pioneer, Cornelius Cane, prepared by him years ago, while the facts were readily obtainable. He has gathered together many interesting and valuable documents, in the course of the years, and these he tendered the writer to make use of in any way he saw fit. The handbill gotten out by Dr. Todd in 1844 advertising for sale certain Indian lands and the town lots of Momence, is an especially prized relic of MT. Buntain's which is reproduced in half-tone.

Mr. Fred Nichols, of Momence, has been indefatigable in his efforts to put the writer in the way of obtaining that data of old days in and about Momence which was most valuable and worthwhile. With his machine and with Clarence Nichols at the wheel, every nook and corner of the old Beaver Lake Basin has been visited, turned wrong-side out and thoroughly scrutinized. Mr. Nichols has been a host in himself.

Hon. Clark Brown, of Union, Missouri, Representative in the Missouri legislature, a former Momence man, by the way, has earned my everlasting gratitude by his unqualified approval of a previous volume and by his timely help in the present one. "The Last Encampment of the Indians," is from the pen of Mr. Brown, in response to a request for something with the touch of the wilderness in it. It is a valuable contribution to the early-day lore of Kankakee county.

O. M. Harlan, of the Press-Reporter, has shown a keen and helpful interest and has supplied data not otherwise obtainable. Mrs. Orra Allen has supplied the details of "Chief White Foot's Home-Coming," a most interesting story. Mrs. Nutt, Mrs. Alzada Hopper, of Momence, and Mr. A. B. Jenkins, of Morocco, Indiana, together with the patriarchal^ Austin Dexter, furnished the details for the story of "Old' Shafer," a character of swamp days whose very name spelled terror for the settlers. Mr. Jenkins, especially, has put me in the way cf many interesting things. He is a gentleman most agreeable and entertaining.

Data concerning Beaver Lake in the days when the hunters sought it, was obtained through Judge W. A. Hunter, of Kankakee, Mr. Victor Brassard, of Momence, Mr. Andy Granger, of DeMotte, Indiana, A. L. Barker, Mr. Lawbaugh.

Joseph Kite, Mr. Nichols, of Lake Village, Indiana, and Mr. A. B. Jenkins, of Morocco, Indiana.

Others who have given valuable aid in one way or another are: Mr. Frank Hamilton, Mr. James Kirby, Mrs. Susan Cook, Mrs. J. H. Freeman, of Momence, Mrs. Lyons, of Sherburnville, E. D. Blakely, Mr. F. O. Chapman and Chas. Sherman, of Kankakee.

BURT E. BURROUGHS.

CONTENTS

INTRODUCTION

MOMENCE OF THE OLD FRONTIER

Momence is an old town—the oldest, perhaps, in north-eastern Illinois bordering on the Illinois-Indiana state-line. She has entered upon the final decade which, on its completion in 1934, will round out one hundred years of existence, speaking by and large. For years it was merely a river settlement without a name, a sort of rallying point for the picturesque southern pioneer hunter, the coureur de bois and voyageur, the Hoosier from the Wabash, and the hard-headed Yankee from Vermont, New Hampshire and New York, whom kindly fortune directed by way of shadowy, indistinct trails to the banks of the Kankakee, in their quest of "wood, water and grass." This spot where the pioneers foregathered is rich in stirring tales of the border. Momence, in her old frontier days, reflected in a marked degree those elemental traits so characteristic of border life. The term, "elemental traits," as applied to the few families Who constituted the population of the old river settlement of the Kankakee ninety years ago and better is relied upon to convey to the reader an idea of the hardihood, self-reliance and independence that possessed them. In that early day there was an absence of repressive measures, no superimposed law except that unwritten law of the border which held a man's property inviolate. A man who stole another's horse in that day knew that he risked his neck. The penalty was death—sure, swift, certain death—once he fell within the clutches of the one who had suffered the loss. The settlement and later the town, after it had emerged from this primitive chrysalis, was for years a reflex of this expansive, unrestricted spirit of the pioneer. Naturally, it was, betimes, an easy-going, wide-

1

open, red-hot, go-as-you-please sort of burg with as varied and nondescript a lot of dwellers, regular and transient, as ever called for whiskey over anybody's bar, or bet their money on a hand of poker or a horse race, or settled their differences man to man with the bare fists.

Momence is the one town on the river that really has a frontier history. Here, in the long ago, where the prairie trails converged to the fords of the Kankakee, ten or a dozen families were attracted, among them the Lacys, the VanKirks, the Hills, the Nichols, the Grahams, the Hayhursts, the Dickeys, the Dutchers, the Buffingtons, in the main representative pioneer stock from Indiana with antecedents harking back to Kentucky, Tennessee, Virginia and the Carolinas. These families settled mainly in the near vicinity of the "Upper Crossing." Nearer the settlement of Momence, a mile away, a stream of eastern people settled. Asher Sargeant was the first to settle there in 1834. In 1835 came his brother, Enoch and a man by the name of McKibben; in 1836 came A. S. Vail, Judge Orson Beebe and Newell Beebe; in 1838 came Daniel Beebe, Caleb Wells and Col. Lyman Worcester; in 1839 came Walter B. Hess, A. B. Parish and Dr. Mazuzan; in 1840 came W. W. Parish, Benjamin Lamport and James Nichols; in 1841 came Dr. David Lynds, James M. Perry, David Perry and Philip Worcester and others. After the lapse of three-quarters of a century, representatives of most of these early-day pioneer families still walk the streets of the old town and are identified with the social and business life of the community.

In 1849, after the bridge had gone out for the second time, "Westport," or "Lorain," as the "Upper Crossing" was variously termed, gave up trying to be a town and gradually added her forces to the struggling backwoods settlement of Momence. So, you see, Momence, as residuary legatee of "Lorain" and her environs, thus falls heir to her traditions, legends and historical lore, and may reasonably lay claim to one hundred years of stirring history.

The Indian was still here when Dr. Todd platted the town. Clad in his blanket, untouched by the civilization about him, he puzzled over the queer actions of the transit man and he who carried the chain and established a multitude of corners by driving stakes here and there. Vaguely he understood that this mysterious process was a mere preliminary to the placing of the white man's tepee. Civilization was knocking at the door of the red- man's domain at last.

The trapper and hunter, the voyageur and coureur de bois, vigorous, hardy, picturesque in his wilderness attire of skins and bright tasseled cap, found a paradise in the upper reaches of the Kankakee, and a game sanctuary in the vast marsh region of nearby Indiana, which thrilled his soul with savage delight. The squatter and the idler rear-ed his abode of logs by the river's side where ever fancy dictated, untroubled by any thought of "meets and bounds," or prior claims. In that early day the universe was his. Here he existed in luxurious idleness surrounded by that plenty which only the wilderness bestows, and thanked God and his lucky stars (if he gave thanks at all), for a situation so charming and soul-satisfying.

During the forties and the fifties, particularly during the fall season and early winter, the hosts of freighters from the Wabash country going to Chicago and back again, made Momence their rendezvous. Mr. W. W. Parish recalls that it was no unusual thing to find as many as one hundred to two hundred teams and wagons disposed along the river at night in camps, while the men, for the most part, filled the saloons and public places of the little settlement and drank and played cards or engaged in conversation as the mood suited. These gatherings represented typical pioneer types. There was the man of the woods, the man of the river, the man of the prairie, every man of them a red-blood-ed individual whom stern necessity and wilderness training had endowed with the quality of looking out for himself anywhere and under any circumstances. Life, for such as these, was a constant hand-to-hand struggle with the elements and hardships an unvarying item in the daily round of experiences. Such were the diverse elements that constituted, in a large measure, the frontier society of that day, and on their visits to the settlement they mingled and jostled and touched elbows in a neighborly, friendly way—the good, the bad, the shiftless and indifferent—in their common meeting place, the saloon or the backwoods grocery, which served quite as well as the saloon if one merely wanted a drink of liquor. The frontier grocery was the forum wherein Democracy thrived in the days when the nation was in the making.

To this rather unpromising composite of frontier types thus thrown together by chance was added in numbers wholly disproportionate to the sum of Momence's population, thieves of high and low degree, counterfeiters, horse thieves and cattle rustlers, who trickled down stream from that impregnable retreat of "Bogus Island," situated in the great "Kankakee Marshes" over the line in Indiana, only fifteen miles away. Eighty years ago, it should be remembered, an organization of desperate men, known as the "Prairie Banditti," operated in the Mississippi Basin. Chiefly their efforts were devoted to stealing horses and making and circulating counterfeit money. They operated from headquarters located in some naturally secluded and inaccessible spot adjacent to the Mississippi river, safe from prying eyes and easily defended. Nauvoo City, of the Mormons, was a favored refuge for certain of the Prairie Banditti for years. Notorious "Dave Redden" had a "run-in" on the river below Davenport, Iowa, where the thief or murderer, hard pressed by the officers of justice, might rest secure from detection. This place was known by the suggestive title of "Devil's Run." St. Louis was a clearing house for stolen horses and there was hardly a horse thief in that day who did not handle spurious coin and pass it at every opportunity.

As their operations grew other natural harbors of security were made use of, notably in the neighborhood of Terre Haute, in the Eel River country of Indiana, on the Wabash and "Bogus Island," situated in the marsh country of Indiana some fifteen miles east of the frontier settlement of Momence. "Bogus Island," with its thousands of acres of open lake, swamp, scrub oak ridges and timber, formed the most perfect rendezvous of all. Thus, it is we find Momence at the very beginning of her career as a backwoods settlement a neighbor of notorious "Bogus Island," and on terms of easy familiarity with the island's habitues. In the course of the years certain members of the squatter and trapper element, easy of conscience and wholly bankrupt as to morals, formed a connection with these island outlaws and served as "spotters," "tip-off men" and purveyors of news generally. A few there were who developed to a point where they could "make a sight" as the location of a desirable horse was termed in outlaw parlance, and also lend valuable aid "in raising the sight," if need be. This squatter "secret service" grew in efficiency as the years went on until its ramifications, penetrating to every quarter, enmeshed the surrounding country until it seemed all but hopeless to prevent a theft, and next to impossible to recover property thus stolen.

Naturally, force was the dominant note in the affairs of men in the days of the old frontier in and about Momence. Such has been the case in all lands and in all places before society crystallized sufficiently to establish law and order. When these men who knew no law let down in the strenuous life, as was often the case, and sought the socia-bility of the border grog shops and gambling dens of the little river town of Momence on the Kankakee, it may well be surmised that "the lid," as we say in this day, was not merely tilted to a comfortable angle, but removed entirely—thrown in the river. Come to think of it, Momence had no such thing as "a lid" until long after these frontier types had passed on. Ah, but those were wild and tumultuous days and nights in the old town 'round about 1849 and for many years thereafter! Coureurs de bois, voyageurs, Indians, trappers, hunters, gamblers, thieves, spotters—all the riff-raff of the wide, wide wilderness mingled indiscriminately in the public houses, all more or less sodden with whiskey. These men of the border who endured much and worked hard, also played hard once the notion struck them.

There were men who, after having spent days in these Bacchanlian orgies, shouldered their packs and hit the up-river trails to some lone cabin set in a bayou, were never heard from again. There were feuds in the old days and the penalty of a wrong was death! The answer to many a

6

disappearance would have been the echo of a rifle shot—a dull splash in the river. The woods never babble of the secrets they hold and the river, undisturbed, flows on and croons of lighter things than death. Only the unfolding of the Judgment Book will solve the mysteries of the upper river of which men talked and gossiped and speculated and then— forgot.

According to the recollection of some of the older citizens Sunday was not observed at all. The saw-mill ran as usual; men went about their vocations while horse races, boxing bouts, foot-races and fights were common Sunday amusements. So absorbed in their own affairs and sports did this border populace become, that they actually lost track of the days of the week and were only reminded of Sunday when the up-river men, who got out timber for Momence's only industry, the saw mill, came down to town in force to spend one big, glad, riotous day in seven. All classes previously mentioned in this heterogeneous mixture of frontier types, regarded the picturesque log-roller with feelings of genuine awe and respect at such times as he invaded their precincts and disported in riotous abandon. Ample leeway at the bar was left for him; the movable articles about the house which would have proved formidable in case of a rough and tumble, were shunted into the clear; the poker game retired to less conspicuous quarters on the appearance of the first installment of visiting "lumber-jacks." Altogether, the action was very much like when a ship battens down her hatches, trims her sails and makes everything safe and snug in the face of an approaching squall.

The frontiersmen tacitly admitted by these acts of precaution that here was a case where an irresistible force was more than likely to come in contact with an immovable body and, to avoid the dire consequences of such a clash, they quietly ebbed to the open spaces of the great out of doors and looked on while the up-river boys took over the place and proceeded to drink themselves "stone-blind." Numerous clashes had taken place between these irreconcilable forces of the frontier, but to no purpose. The riverman, cocky and smiling, flaunted his challenge in the face and eyes of all comers. His very presence in town was an invitation to fight. And, when he fought, he was a human wild-cat who observed no law or rule but considered any means fair that enabled him to vanquish his opponent.

The town boys recalled only too bitterly that their champion came out of the last set-to with a thumb "chawed off," or nearly so, and with one ear elongated and drooping for all the world like that of a "pot-lickin' hound." And, supposedly, there were rules, agreed to beforehand, governing this fight, which Queensberry himself would have approved of. Decidedly they were a bad lot and not to be trusted. For years the question of supremacy was an open one with the odds laying noticeably in the direction of "up-river." In the vernacular of the old town of the border at a time when polished phrase languished in the background and only vigorous, resounding superlative thrived, these rivermen were characterized as "an ornery, low-lived set, of the damndest, most orneriest stripe!" With this high and lofty declaration, those who were wont to make the old town ring with the echoes of their noisy carousal and mad pranks during six days and nights of the week, quietly relinquished their places on the seventh day and—the sad truth must be admitted— hunted their holes.

They were gainers in one respect, however. While the ancient Chaldeans reckoned their time from the stars, these old-town people reckoned theirs from the day the rivermen "got through raisin' hell!" That day was always Monday, but the count was often hopelessly mixed by the time next Sunday arrived. Do you wonder that Momence had a bad name? Do you marvel that the leaven of good as represented by the few God-fearing families of the neighborhood took so long to permeate the mass and leaven the whole lump?

Time, no less than nature, works his wonders. The softening influence of time is easily discerned in the old town of today. There is a noticeable polish, an air of dignity, an unmistakable refinement, an all-pervading prosperousness that conveys a charming sense of poise, serenity and general well-being. Decidedly the passing years have not been unkind. But, at mention of her wild and woolly days, methinks she stirs uneasily and lifts a hand deprecatingly as if to say: "Now, for Heaven's sake, do be careful! The past is gone; the past is dead—why trouble to dig it up?" Why dig it up indeed? Only that sometimes one travels far from the beaten paths of home to sense the atmosphere of old days; to glimpse the red-blood spirit of the frontier before the iron had been leached from it; to hob-knob with the shades of those erstwhile giants who, standing on the threshold of civilization, acknowledged God yet feared no man.

Momence, then, had all the elements that went to make a border town. She had all the color, action and picturesqueness so characteristic of border days when law was a myth, restraint unknown and whose best man, picked from the varied types of the wilderness, was admitted to be he who could swear the loudest, hit the hardest, drink the most liquor and owned the best "race hoss." By degrees we have sought to bring the reader to a realization that Momence, way, way back, in the times of the brush and the big timber, was about as tough as the toughest of them. The fact that it was tough is not a pleasing recommendation altogether. It should not be gathered from these remarks that we would glorify the fact unduly. No, indeed! We are content to follow in the wake of others who have served mankind by immortalizing the bold deeds of the border in song, and verse, and story. Therefore, to this end, the shades of old-time traditions, once rich and colorful that still lurk, phantom-like, on the borderland of memory—faded, shadowy, indistinct in the deepening twilight of oblivion, have been besought to tell their story—just this once.

"THE UPPER CROSSING ON THE KANKAKEE"

> "So, come, good men who toil and tire,
> Who smoke and sip the kindly cup,
> Ring round about the tavern fire
> Ere yet you drink your liquor up;
> And hear my simple tales of earth,
> Of youth and truth and living things;
> Of poverty and proper mirth,
> Of rags and rich imaginings."
>
> —ROBERT W. SERVICE.

There is no spot in all eastern Illinois more redolent of memories of frontier days than that spot known as the "Metcalf Farm," situated one mile east of the present city of Momence on the Kankakee River. Here the first white settlement in Eastern Illinois took place as far back as ninety years ago, all because a well-defined Indian trail dipped down the north bank to the river and emerged again on the south bank, indicating to the solitary trapper with his pack or the lone pioneer traveler with his ox team that here was a safe and convenient ford. Scarcely a mile away to the southwest on the river where the city of Momence of today is located, were two other fords thirty rods apart where the limestone "hog-back" of the river bed lifted sufficiently to make transportation easy and safe. Three ideal fording places located within a mile was something very unusual. Nature truly was prodigal with her favors in this as well as other respects. A convenient river ford in the old wilderness days was quite as important an adjunct to a locality as the railroad afterwards became. All lines of travel north and south of the river converged towards this segment of the Kankakee with

11

its three fords. Chicago was the objective of the frontiersman from the Danville country, from the region of Vincennes, Indiana, and the Wabash country of central Indiana. During the thirties, the forties and the early fifties the stream of travel to and from the growing metropolis of Chicago grew in volume. Mainly these travelers used the ford nearest the Indiana state-line and called it the "Up-per Crossing," thus distinguishing it from the two farther west at Momence.

In March of 1831, when Cook county was organized, its southern boundary was the Kankakee River and its eastern boundary the Indiana state-line. In the year 1833 Chicago voted to incorporate as a village, and in the fall of that same year the settlement at "Upper Crossing" was inaugurated. The first house built in what is now eastern Kankakee county was on the farm since owned by Silas Metcalf, located on the north side of the river. It was a log house and was situated east of the present orchard. It was built by William Lacy. Lacy came from Danville, Illinois, with James VanKirk, who drove from Danville settlement to Chicago with a load of produce.

The quartering of a large number of soldiers in Chicago incident to the Black Hawk war, made provisions scarce and dear at that point and this induced VanKirk and Lacy to brave the privations and dangers of an overland trip through the almost unknown country. Both VanKirk and Lacy were deeply impressed with the beauty and natural advantages of this site on the Kankakee and, on their return, they stopped. As related, Lacy built the cabin on the Metcalf place and staid there during the winter. Mr. VanKirk started a cabin on the head of the island nearby and carried up the walls almost to the roof when he departed. He expected to return the following year and perfect his claim but, for some reason did not do so. Lacy sold his claim a year or two later and thus failed to become a permanent resident of the settlement of which he was the founder.

During the course of the years the settlement at "Upper Crossing" attracted a dweller now and then until by 1845, it is said, there were as many as ten or a dozen families located there whose numbers were about evenly divided between the north and south banks of the river. During these years "Upper Crossing" was variously known as "Westport," "Hill's Ford," and later, when Dr. David Lynds was given the post office, as "Lorain." There is a wide difference of opinion or memory as to the old settlement. By some it is contended that there was scarcely anything there besides the tavern, while others are equally positive that there were twelve to fifteen houses on the two sides of the river. There were several stores in the early days. Elon Curtis clerked in one of them, a place kept by a man by the name of Glover. Allen Rakestraw, widely known as "Old Dime," from his closeness in financial matters, kept a dram shop. There was also a blacksmith shop. The father of Dr. M. D. Green was also the gunsmith. Louis Buffington kept a tailor shop. Joseph VanKirk kept a hotel on the north side of the river for a while. The old settlers of Yellowhead maintain that it was the principal trading point from about 1840 to 1848 and, in that event, it must have been quite a hamlet. The place had a bridge, built in 1842 which lasted until 1846. Another was built which went out in the spring of 1849.

In 1834 Asher Sargeant built the first habitation, a double log cabin at the island ford a mile to the southwest of the "Upper Crossing" and thus unconsciously acquired fame as the original settler of the present-day municipality of Momence.

He was the first store keeper at this point for, in one-half of the cabin, he established a small grocery whose principal articles of trade were whiskey and tobacco. As Newell Beebe expressed it, "they were the cheap products of the country." Asher Sargeant was followed by his brother Enoch, who came in 1835 accompanied by a man by the name of McKibben. These three, then, were the original first settlers at Momence, within the present city limits.

The double log house erected by Asher Sargeant, as nearly as can be ascertained at this late day, stood somewhere between the old Worcester and Lane hall and the residence of P. J. Cleary, probably where the alley now id between Range and Pine streets, just north of the river.

As there were neither roads nor streets nor alleys in that day its exact location would now be difficult to determine. There seems to have been a question in the minds of the older settlers as to the year Asher Sargeant built his cabin on the Kankakee. John Smith, of Sherburnville, says that he came to this region with his parents in October, 1835, crossing the river at the present site of Momence. They stopped with Asher Sargeant who was living in the house at that time. He thinks 1834 is the probable date of its erection.

Asher Sargeant also built a saw-mill nearby. Some think the saw-mill was the first building put up. It is quite certain, however, that the saw-mill was not built until 1837 or 1838. Mr. Smith says the saw-mill was not there at the time of his arrival. William Parish says that the Sargeant house had "puncheon" or hewed floors, which would not have been the case had Sargeant built the mill first.

Mr. Parish had a lively recollection of attending a dance at the Sargeant home and of getting splinters in his bare feet from the floor while dancing. The cotillion was halted while William sat down and extracted them. Several deep-seated slivers required the services of his lady to successfully extract, whereupon the dance was resumed.

About 1838, Asher Sargeant erected as a matter of fact, the first mill for grinding corn in this part of the country. This mill was built on the farm now owned by John H. Nichols, one and a half miles northeast of Momence, on Trim Creek. The site was about a half mile east of Hubbard's trail, and a mile north of Hill's Tavern and the location of the first post office, Lorain. A dam was built across the creek to hold water for power, and a canal was dug about 80 rods from a bend in the creek to the mill. This canal is plainly to be seen today. Also, some of the timbers of the old dam such as mud-sills are embedded in the bottom of the creek and are in a good state of preservation. The mill was abandoned about the time the mill was erected in Momence in 1843, on account of lack of power. The grinding buhrs were cast aside and laid near the road for years, finally being sold and taken to Lowell, Indiana, where they were used in a mill for years.

The second house to be built in Momence was also a log structure but the name of the builder is lost to us. Matt Anderson and Isaac. Gray lived in it, however, while they were employed at the saw-mill.

Oliver Beebe sat in this chair and drove his team from Vermont to the Kankakee. He was an uncle of judge Orson Beebe. The board in the center is what is Known as a "Shake." Judge Orson Beebe placed it there to rest his head on when he slept. There is a tradition that Governor Skinner, of Vermont, once owned it. It is now in the Possession of Miss Lucy Day of Redlands, California.

In 1836 A. S. Vail and Orson Beebe, who came to the Beebe Grove settlement near Crete, Illinois, in 1835, moved on to the Kankakee. As they surmounted the hill north of Momence Mr. Vail, enraptured by the marvelous panorama of plains and woods through which the river took its leisurely, winding way, exclaimed: "Here is where I stay!" There was the ring of prophesy in his words. He lived to see the wilderness of that day give way to beautiful homes and growing crops. A kindly providence vouchsafed to him the rare privilege of living to be a centenarian— almost. To him, by natural selection, perhaps, fell the honor of being the town's historian and arbiter of moot questions of names and dates and facts involving the settlers thereabouts. How rare a quality is that which remembers when most of the world forgets! His rare memory supplied the newspaper man with many a story of old days now and then. The high school student of later days sought him out and chronicled in an essay or school paper some interesting experience of wilderness days. At public gatherings, when the pioneers came together, "Uncle Sid" was the moving spirit, the recognized leader in ra counting those interesting experiences with which the lives of the pioneers were filled.

Save for a chance newspaper article that has survived, a high school year book, found now and then, with data of the past preserved therein, the memory of the older citizens who enjoyed the rare privilege of listening to "Uncle Sid" Vail constitutes the only source of information in this day. Oh, that some early-day scribe with note-book and pencil had shadowed "Uncle Sid" and recorded his utterances with the same persistent fidelity with which Boswell pursued Dr. Johnson.

17

The third house built in Momence was on the south side of the river and was put up by A. S. Vail and Judge Orson Beebe. It was located a few rods west of where the Chicago & Eastern Illinois railroad bridge now is, not far from the South channel of the river. It was a double log cabin of goodly dimensions and, on its completion, the builders engaged in the tavern business. Theirs was the first regularly established tavern in Momence.

Mr. Vail and Mr. Beebe bought the land on which the business section of Momence stands today for $220 in gold. They held possession of this tract for eight years and then lost it by a "float." The peculiar designation of "float" was applied to certain awards of land to members of the Prairie Band of the Pottawattomi under the treaty of 1833, whereby they ceded their lands generally to the United States. Those Indians to whom a land award was made by the government, had the privilege of making their selection wherever they chose after the survey of these lands had been completed, provided, of course, that the land thus chosen had not been previously entered. This privilege was what was termed "a float title." The claim purchased by Mr. Vail and Mr. Beebe had been guaranteed to be free from "floats," but it was afterwards ascertained that an Indian "float" had been located on the land. In consequence of this they lost their claims and the only benefit they derived from eight years' occupation of the land was the use of it and the house which stood upon it.

The first frame house built within the present limits of Momence was by Chauncey Chipman, probably about the year 1841 or 1842. As nearly as can be ascertained now it was erected on the east side of Range street, not far from Second, probably on the lot owned by N. Cantway, north of the old

Knighthart livery stable. In the opinion of Newell Beebe, it was the fourth house to be built within the present limits. It was built before Dr. Todd platted the town of Momence. L. D. Edwards, who came here in 1843, says that the house was standing then and is the same house that now stands on the lot. This, then, is the oldest house in Momence, the prior log structures having long since disappeared.

Messrs. Vail and Beebe did a good business with their tavern notwithstanding only a 26 mile away at the "Upper Crossing," the famous Boniface, Robert Hill, held forth at "Hill's Tavern." Prior to 1833 and up until the late sixties these fords were made use of by the settlers in, Eastern Illinois south of the river and those of south-western Indiana who hauled their produce to Chicago. Year by year this travel was augmented by thousands of immigrants moving into the west. Mr. Parish says that he has beheld more than a hundred wagon outfits camped on the river at Momence in a single evening. It was a delightful spot in the old days and, apparently, caught the fancy of all who came that way.

About 1845 a good deal of travel from central western Indiana began to be diverted from the "Upper Crossing" to Momence by way of still another ford on the Kankakee, that known as "The Day Ford," situated a mile or two north-east of the village of Aroma Park. Principally these were frontier farmers from Indiana hauling their produce to Chicago who found they were thus enabled to avoid many miles of heavy, sandy road, by cutting across the Chicago-Vincennes Road to this ford where they crossed the Kankakee and followed the trail around to Momence. In the course of the years many hundreds of teams came by this route.

Luther Gleason tells an interesting story of the days when he was a little boy living on the prairie farm that fronted the river in the segment between Aroma Park and East Court Street bridge, not far from the "Day Ford." Many Indiana farmers used to cross here on their way to Chicago with loads of apples. It was along in 1848 during the Zachary Taylor campaign, and the older members of the family used to put him up to hurrah for Taylor at such times as the apple wagons passed by. The result was that Taylor being very popular as a presidential candidate among the Indianaians, they would invariably throw out a liberal quantity of apples as they passed in evidence of friendly appreciation. Mr. Gleason says that one day a lone apple wagon came by and, after he had duly hurrahed for Taylor, the driver of the team stopped suddenly and asked: "what for?" And the boy, somewhat abashed and confused at the unexpected query, replied truthfully but haltingly, "For Apples."

"Upper Crossing," be it known, was famous in a way long before William Lacy and James VanKirk settled there in 1833. The "Crossing," so far as the white man's activities are concerned, dates back into the gray shadows of the past for more than a century. If Momence citizens were disposed to take advantage of the opportunity thus presented to stress the historical importance of the place as well as that of deserted "Upper Crossing" at the Metcalf farm, they could give us an historical pageant that would be well worth anyone's time to witness.

That "Iron Man" of the frontier, Gurdon S. Hubbard, together with Noel LeVasseur, Dominique Bray, Victor Porthier, Jacques Jombeaux, Antoine Bourbonnais and others inaugurated the "Hubbard Trace" between the little trading post of "Bunkum," on the Iroquois river, and South Water Street, which is only another name for Chicago of the frontier. This was done in the year 1824, more than one hundred years ago, nine years before the settlement at "the Crossing" in 1833. The "Hubbard Trace" made use of this crossing. It was a day when the Indian villages of the Pottawattomi, hunters, trappers and traders with their strings of pack-horses, coureurs du bois and an occasional voyageur clad in the picturesque attire of the border, crossed and recrossed the Kankakee at this ford.

This famous trail, first blazed by Gurdon S. Hubbard from Chicago one hundred and fifty miles south-east of Danville, was later used in part when the Illinois State Assembly authorized the Chicago-Vincennes Road to be located in 1833-4. That part of the road north from Danville to Chicago was followed by the commissioners with but little variation, for the line was direct and followed the high ground. The Assembly ordered this road to be marked, at intervals of one mile with numbered milestones, beginning at Vincennes. Probably the only stone now extant between Danville and Chicago is that which now stands in front of the John Nichols home two miles north of "Upper Crossing." It is the 179th milestone. It is in a good state of preservation and has been guarded with jealous care by the Nichols family for many years. For years this stone stood in the field and was subsequently removed to the roadside, a few rods to the west.

This "Trace" instituted by Hubbard in 1824 furnished a much more direct and convenient method of communication between the posts of the fur country and headquarters at Chicago. By means of the pack-horse the season's furs were easily transported, whereas before, the pack had been freighted out by means of boats. Traversing the Iroquois and the Kankakee to the DesPlaines was not so bad, generally, but in times of low water in the DesPlaines and "Mud Lake," the men were often obliged to work all day in water up to their waists. Transporting supplies to and from the interior by this primitive means was an exhausting, heart-breaking experience at best. From 1824 as long as Hubbard operated in the country, every pelt from the Iroquois and the Kankakee and the nearby Indiana marshes, went into Chicago on the back of a pack-horse.

In the winter of 1830-31, a winter remembered among the pioneers for its heavy snow and intense cold, Hubbard undertook to drive a bunch of hogs which he had picked up along the trail from Danville to old "Bunkum," to Chicago. There was snow on the ground to the depth of seven inches when he started. It took him several days to reach the "Upper Crossing on the Kankakee with his herd. He pitched his camp on the south bank in a hollow that afforded some protection from the wind. The snow was slushy and a fine rain had set in as the men turned in for the night During the night it turned colder and, on awakening in the morning the men found their clothing frozen fast to the ground so that they extricated themselves with difficulty. It was very cold and snowing heavily, so the hogs were rounded up in the deep snow in the hollow where the men had bivouaced and left to shift for themselves.

Hubbard crossed the river and went in search of Chief Yellowhead's camp up at the present Yellowhead Point, which he was successful in finding in spite of the storm which raged furiously.

AN ANCIENT MILE-STONE

About the only Remaining Stone Which Marked the Chicago-Vincennes Trail in 1834. It is Stone 179, and Stands Opposite the Home of Mrs. Malinda Nichols, Northeast of Momence.

Here also he found his old friend, the half-breed, Billy Caldwell, a brother-in-law of Yellowhead, who had his tepee pitched close by. Hubbard was welcomed by Caldwell with true aboriginal hospitality, and during the two days that the storm raged he remained, meanwhile drinking prodigious quantities of tea brewed by Caldwell's squaw.

When the drive with the hogs was again resumed the snow was two feet deep on a level, and in some places had drifted over the trail to a depth of five or six feet. The wagons that carried the feed for the animals broke out a partial trail but the drifts had to be shoveled out Naturally progress was slow.

Hubbard said that it took Thirty Days to go from the Kankakee river to Chicago with that drove of hogs, such being the difficulties encountered on the way. He slaughtered such as remained of the herd on his arrival in Chicago and disposed of the carcasses.

On the return trip it took ten days to come as far as the "Upper Crossing" on the Kankakee. The ice and drifts and the cold were so great as to thus impede the progress of empty wagons. Again, they were obliged to shovel their way through great drifts to enable the wagons to pass. It was a bitter night when the Kankakee was reached. The river was high and filled with floating ice. The great box of the Pennsylvania wagon was removed and its openings chinked with snow over which water was poured which froze instantly and made it water tight. Harness, blankets and utensils were loaded into this improvised boat and, with the men, were safely transferred to the opposite bank. But the horses had to swim for it. Altogether, the time consumed for that round trip from "Bunkum" post on the Iroquois to Chicago and

24

back, a distance of about one hundred and fifty miles, was near fifty days. While that constitutes pretty nearly a record for time consumed in making a short trip, the outstanding feature is the spirit of hardihood on the part of those who persevered and by sheer endurance and grit triumphed finally over the elements.

The hogs that made up this drove of Hub-bard's in 1830 were not comparable to those marketed in this day. As a pioneer expressed it, those old-time hogs were range hogs and used to hustling for a living. They were large in body, with long legs and seldom or never fat. Apparently, they were built for speed and endurance, and at that not all of the herd with which Hubbard started for Chicago, survived the hardships of the trip. Necessity was the spur by which our pioneer fathers were urged to attempt the unusual. Hardship and personal discomfort and suffering did not particularly matter IF THE THING COULD BE DONE.

That piece of road which leads from the river bank on the north side passing the Metcalf home and continuing north for thirty or forty rods to the Buntain corner, is actual Hubbard Trail, in the main. It is historic ground. For most people the imagination fails in its efforts to picture the strange frontier types that thronged it in the early twenties and thirties. For the most part the enormous import of that slow-moving panorama in which is pictured the ox teams and covered wagons of the forties and fifties, is lost to us today. But the fact remains that the "Upper Crossing," deserted though it is in this day and devoid of even the semblance of a settlement, was the gateway through which those builders of the great middle west thronged.

THE NAMING OF MOMENCE

As a matter of fact, Momence was named eighty-one years ago, ten years after Asher Sargeant drifted in over the lower ford and reared the first white man's habitation within the present city limits. This spot which was destined to become Momence, although attracting a settler now and then, had no name at all from 1834 up until 1841 or 1842. In one or the other of those years A. S. Vail received the appointment as postmaster and, as a name for the office then became an absolute necessity, he christened the office "Lorain," in honor of his sister-in-law, Miss Lorain Beebe, sister of Judge Orson Beebe and Newell Beebe. This first post office of Lorain was kept in a small building which Mr. Vail also used as a residence, located west of the present Paradis wagon shops not far from the river between Front Street and River Street.

The ford at the Metcalf farm a mile east was much more fortunate in the matter of distinguishing titles. Originally it was known as the "Upper Crossing," "Hill's Ford," "Westport" and later as "Lorain" when congressman "Long John" Wentworth, on discovering that Mr. Vail was a Whig, searched out the only democrat in the community capable of conducting the office, Dr. David Lynds, and made him postmaster. Dr. Lynds lived in the near vicinity of the "Upper Crossing," somewhere near to where the Tiffany Brick Works are today, and, after his appointment he moved the office to his home. The name "Lorain" could not be improved upon in the opinion of the Doctor, for he had become the husband of Miss Lorain Beebe in the meantime.

This sale bill, gotten out in 1844, by Dr.Hiram Todd, advertised lots in the new townsite of Momence for sale.

So, forsaking all other titles by which the settlement at the "Upper Crossing" had been known since 1833, it gladly blossomed out as "Lorain," and by that name it is known unto this day by the older inhabitants. The incipient settlement only a mile away, first known as "Lorain," thus robbed of its importance, waited in nameless-obscurity for that great event—a real birth as an industrial community which took place in 1844.

Regarding the name "Momence," there has been a notable conflict of opinion regarding its origin among the elders of the community. It is strange how the important details of this backwoods christening failed to register in the memory of that day. Hiram W. Beckwith, of Danville, who is well known for his writings of the early history of the state and especially Eastern Illinois, says the name Momence was derived from "Momenza," a noted Pottawattomie chief, the assumption being that a clerk in the office of Indian affairs at Washington after wrestling in vain with the undecipherable hand writing thus expressed it. On the other hand, A. S. Vail, who knew the Indian personally, says that his name was "Mo-ness." Dr. Hiram Todd, of Rockville, Illinois, who platted the original townsite of Momence in 1844, and advertised the same in 1845 by means of posters (a photographic reproduction of one of which is hereby given), states specifically that "The proprietors have recently laid out a town which they have called MOMENCE, THE NAME OF THE ORIGINAL INDIAN RESERVEE!"

What a conflict of eminent authorities! Dr. Todd, however, was a careful, methodical man of business, a lawyer and an Associate Judge of the Cass county, Indiana Circuit. From 1833 to 1843 he had become the purchaser of eight thousand acres of Indian Reservation and "Grant lands" on the Kankakee river from Rock Creek to Momence. He must have been well informed as to the particular treaty of 1832 by means of which the United States government came into possession of the lands of the Prairie Band of the Pottawattomi as well as those of the Pottawattomi of lower Michigan and upper Indiana, of which "To-pen-ne-bee" was the head chief and "Po-ka-gon" second chief. The treaty itself throws interesting light on the situation since it mentions specifically the names of all Indian members to whom "floating grants" of land were made. The Frenchman, Pierre Moran, alias "Peerish," was a chieftain of power and influence in the band of which To-pen-ne-bee was the head. His half-breed son, "Mo-ness," was a chief by reason of having married "Je-neir," the daughter of a chief. "Je-neir," under the treaty, was given a floating grant for one section of land. The three half-breed sons of Pierre Moran were given a total of one section disposed as follows: to "Wa-be-ga," and "Isadore Mo-mence," one-quarter section each; to "Saw-grets," one half section. It is a significant fact that "Mo-ness," the husband of "Je-neir," was not awarded a foot of land under this treaty.

A popular historical tradition, however, credits "Mo-ness" with having received two and one-half sections of land and that on the 31st of July 1834, he gave a bond to execute a deed for this "float" to one James R. McCord. By many it is thought that McCord located the "float" where Momence stands today. McCord never got his deed but, instead, sold his claim to Todd & Bainbridge, May 13,

1843. One thing is evident; "Mo-ness," beyond a doubt gave a bond for a deed to somebody's "float title," probably the section awarded to his squaw, "Je-neir." It seems hardly probable that he took it upon himself to transfer the holdings of his three brothers, amounting in all to one section. We repeat, it seems unlikely that this was done, although many curious transactions involving the Indian and the white man have come to light now and then which afforded a basis for serious legal complications and long drawn out litigation. This, unfortunately, happened in the case of the titles to the land upon which Momence now stands.

The survey of the townsite of Momence was inaugurated during the summer of 1844 by Dr. Hiram Todd. W. A. Chatfield was at that time building the flouring mill on the island. Twelve blocks were laid out in this first survey, bounded on the north by Fourth Street, on the east by Maple Street, on the south by River Street and on the west by Range Street. This survey was made by Robert J. Boylan, of Joliet, in 1844. Joseph Webster, later a resident of Momence, carried the chain and drove the stakes. The townsite of Momence was opened for sale to the public April 22,1845, large posters of that date, signed by Hiram Todd, announcing the fact to the public at large. It is a significant fact that the name of the town is given in the bills as "Momence." The plat of the townsite was entered of record at Joliet, Will county, in 1846 as "Momence."

Mr. Isaac Olds, who worked on the Chat- field mill in 1844, gives testimony regarding the naming of Momence that is incontrovertible. He says: "Dr. Todd gave the name of Momence to the town. I remember that he was talking about it and at the time proposed two names, "Momence" and "Sawgrets," as nearly as I can remember. Mrs. Chatfield, who was present, said: "Doctor, why don't you call the place

Toddsville?" He refused the suggestion and finally settled upon the name "Momence." This illuminating statement by Mr. Olds clears up several points that have been more or less controversial in the town's history. First—the names of "Momence" and "Saw-grets," between which Dr. Todd hesitated in a matter of selection, are the names of two half-breed sons of the chieftain Pierre Moran who received "floating grants" to land under the same treaty as the squaw "Je-neir. Second—in the volume of Indian treaties, published by the United States Government in 1837, on page 543, the last paragraph contains the names "Isadore Mo-mence and "Saw- grets," sons of "Pier Moran." The name Momence, then, was not a coined name as many believed. The name as given to the town by Dr. Todd and later to the township, appeared in the treaty in the exact othography of today, barring the elimination of the hyphen after the first syllable.

Some years later, when the township of Ganeer was struck off from Momence township, it was thought to be the proper thing to name it after the original grantee, the squaw Je-neir, whose "floating grant" of one section adjoined on the west that of Pierre Moran's three half-breed sons, "Wa-be-ga," "Isadore Mo-mence" and "Saw-grets." These sections were divided by the range line and Range Street which divides the city thus derives its significance. Clark Richards, who made the first survey and plat of the township, entered the name as "Ganeer." It went on record that way and no effort ever was made to rectify this lapse in the expressed orthography of the treaty of 1832.

It was a worthy sentiment, however, on the part of those old-time residents of Momence that sought to unite this ancient aboriginal couple in this way and preserve for all time the historical associations suggested by the names "Momence and "Je-neir." But, by that peculiar fatuity which led them to regard "Mo-ness" as "Mo-men-za," and finally "Momence," they have fallen short of achieving the thing they sought. As matters stand, the aged "Mo-ness is in total eclipse; the youthful half-breed "Momence" is holding hands, so to speak, across an imaginary line with his sister-in-law, "Je-neir," or "Ganeer," in modern parlance, and to use a phrase of the late Stephen R. Moore—"and there you are!"

Isaac Olds bought the first town lot sold in Momence in 1845. It was the one on which Thomas Hamilton afterwards built. He paid thirty dollars for it. The United States, it is said, did not make a deed to "Mo-ness" until February 17,1845, and it does not appear that "Mo-ness" ever executed anything but the bond for a deed. Things went on in this manner until April 29, 1853. At this time Johnathan Crews, a man who lived by looking up defective Indian titles went to Arkansas and got a deed to the entire tract from an Indian who claimed to be the son and only living heir of Mo-ness and Je-neir.

Crews interested Lycurgus Sherman, a banker of LaPorte, Indiana, and others in his title, and then began the war over rival titles to the land on which Momence was located, that resulted so disastrously to the growth and development of the town. There were others angles to this mix-up of titles which tended to involve the situation with so many complexities that the matter was taken to the United States Court.

As a result of this action the United States Court on December 18, 1864, issued an order which perpetually enjoined Crews, Sherman, et al, from interfering in any way with the James Mix titles, acquired through Todd & Bainbridge.

On January 16, 1865, a special deed was given Mix by Henry W. Brooks, special Commissioner appointed by the United States Court. Then, for the first time, Momence property owners became sure of their titles after ten' years of litigation and uncertainty. Mix paid the Crews faction $1,000 in consideration of the settlement and a quit-claim deed. On account of the many flaws contained in the early record, and the fact that the United States Court made the title good in 1864, few abstracts run back beyond that date, and in most cases, Mix made new deeds to the property already sold.

From 1845 up until the advent of Crews with his rival townsite in 1853, Momence enjoyed a considerable growth. Of the older inhabitants who have been prominent in the town's business history, most of them came here between the years 1849 and 1853. M. A. Atherton, Slocum Wilbur, J. L. Clark and perhaps a dozen more settled in the town between those dates. The same may be said of fully a dozen more who have moved away or gone to their long homes. The return of the post- office from Lorain occurred in the spring of 1849, and the changing of the name to Momence, apparently marked the real beginning of Momence as a municipality

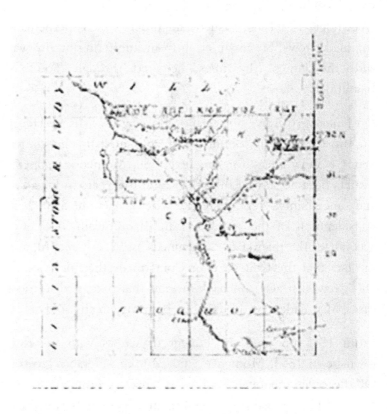

This is a Reproduction of the First Map Ever Made of Kankakee County. It was Made by Clark Richards. It was Made in 1852 and Shows the. Old Trail Which' ran From the Southeast to the Northwest Through the City of Kankakee. Iroquois County at that Time Came to the Kankakee River on the South, and Will County on the North.

THE PASSING OF "OLD TRAPPER DAN"

Better than sixty years ago, the Kankakee river from Momence eastward to the state-line was a paradise for the trapper who sought fine furs. It was more than a paradise for the fisherman—it was Heaven, that's all! It was a favored spot for that unique character of the frontier, the restless, roving coureur de bois who, charmed by the plentitude of nature's charms in this particular section, stayed on and on until the tradition of the rover had given way completely to that of the peaceful, contented, easy-going habitant.

In this early day, before the natural beauty of the river had been defaced or distorted by the so-called "improvements of growing civilization," there appeared one day an old campaigner, black with the grime of the wilderness and with but little of this world's goods, who, in his summing up of the beauty of the situation unconsciously paid tribute to omnipotence when he said: "God only made one country like this, and he made it for me!" This is no idle, extravagant statement, in proof of which we cite the fact that here, years ago, that staunch old pioneer Dan Parmlee, located "The Garden of Eden," after having traversed many countries and many climes.

Poor, old, eccentric Dan! He was not so far off in the naming the place at that. And how he loved it! His castle was a rude hut but a castle none the less. A narrow "draw" which ran from the river inland for a distance of one hundred feet or more enabled him to bring his canoe right up to the door of a log store-house in which he stored his furs. And here, at times when he felt the symptoms of those peculiar "loco" spells, with which he was later in life beset, he shut himself in

35

with the furs for a week at a time, a voluntary prisoner on his own domain.

In time, trouble came to Dan, trouble not of his own making. But whether you make your own trouble or have it made for you it is trouble just the same. "The Garden of Eden" was mortgaged. It was a new phase of life for Dan whose independent nature rebelled at paying interest, to say nothing of the principal. In the course of the years, this man who refused to take civilization seriously, was haunted by the spectre of a bailiff with foreclosure papers. The bailiff, in turn, was haunted by the vision of old "Dan" himself armed with that long-range rifle of his which was never known to miss a target at one hundred yards. There was an uncompromising air about this tall, lean, gaunt backwoods figure, a set expression about the chin and the lower jaw, a peculiar hardness of the pale blue eyes by which one knew instinctively that all overtures for mercy (especially on the part of a bailiff) would prove fruitless and unavailing.

In the end, the vision of the man with the rifle and the high-set chin prevailed. Eventually Dan did what he said he was going to do, sometime—"die there by God!" At his passing the tidings of the old man's death were first brought to Momence by one of his own kith and kin who, sauntering into the old stone saloon on Range street, responded first to an invitation from the boys to take a drink, after which he startled the company by the sententious query: "Didyuh hear the news?" They had not, of course. "The old man's dead," he announced with all the assurance of one who gives important news first. "Why, the devil you say," exclaimed one of the crowd.

TRAPPER DAN PARMLEE

A Familiar Early-Day Character About Momence who had his Abode at "The Garden of Eden," Up-river Between Momence and the Indiana State-line.

"Yes, I do," he ejaculated, "he's deader 'en hell—died last night; if you don't believe me ask Melby; been diggin' a grave up t' Sherurnville. Funeral 's goin' to be this afternoon."

Although it was in the dead of winter and exceedingly cold, the boys of the old frontier town proved themselves loyal to the memory of the old trapper and turned out in force. It was a cold, dreary drive over frozen roads that were rough and bumpy, first to the "Garden of Eden," where the remains of Old Dan were loaded onto a wagon, and thence to the cemetery at Sherburnville. On arriving at the cemetery, a single glance at the undisturbed snow-clad surface disclosed the fact that no grave had, as yet, been dug. After a short deliberation it was decided to dig one then and there. Men cleared with their feet a space in the snow and then gathered timber from the nearby woods and made a roaring fire. This was made necessary from the fact that the ground was frozen to a depth of two and a half to three feet and was as hard as steel.

So, the wood was piled on, and while the process of thawing out the ground was going on, the friends of Old Dan gathered close and absorbed the genial heat and thawed out also, and when their chattering teeth had been stilled sufficiently to admit of coherent speech, the things they said about the man who had fallen down in the funeral arrangements were hardly fit for a respectable barroom, to say nothing of a solemn occasion such as a funeral.

The work of thawing out the ground and digging the grave consumed much time, during which the members of the funeral party worked in shifts, carrying wood for the fire or taking a hand at the spade.

The grave was finished at last, not a grave of regulation depth, but sufficient under the circumstances, so the crowd thought, and the remains of the old trapper were deposited therein. The commitment of "dust to dust" is always a solemn act whether the body goes shriven or unshriven into eternal rest, and a hush fell upon the little group huddled about the yawning grave. After a pause, they looked one to another, awkwardly, inquiringly, not knowing just what was expected of them in the emergency, and then, one by one they removed their hats as if by a common impulse and for a moment bared their heads to the chilling blast, while the winter winds intoned a requiem in the tops of the nearby woods.

"UNCLE BILLY" NICHOLS COLLECTS FOR A HAM

Grandfather William Nichols, known throughout the community of Momence as "Uncle Billy," was a square-toed, upstanding individual whose reputation for truth, veracity and square-dealing was proverbial. He was a powerful man physically, standing six feet four in his stocking feet, of the lean, rangy type, and, notwithstanding his genial, urbane manner, was a dangerous individual to try and "run a sandy on," as they sometimes used to do in the old days of the frontier. Johnnie Marshall, who used to run a saloon on the west side of Range street, three or four doors south of the corner, bought a ham from "Uncle Billy" one day, a regular honest-to- goodness old fashioned, sugar-cured smokehouse ham such as everybody used to have in the days before they ever dreamed of painting them with "liquid smoke." The ham was duly delivered and in the course of a week or two "Uncle Billy" dropped into Marshall's place to collect for it.

Marshall's place was a one-story frame building something over fifty feet in length which stood, in the opinion of many of the older citizens, about where the Parish bank is today. The Marshall saloon was a popular place in its day. The distinguishing feature of the building was its floor. That floor conveyed to the casual visitor a sense of primitive antiquity as nothing else could. This floor was laid with elegant black walnut slabs twelve feet in length, three inches thick and from eighteen to twenty-four inches in width! Can you imagine it? These black walnut slabs were the product of the local saw-mill in a day when virgin timber was drawn upon without stint. In the early days white oak lumber was more highly esteemed than walnut and who knows but that the saw-mill man may have congratulated himself on "putting over" something clever when he unloaded this bunch of walnut for Johnnie Marshall's floor instead of good, white oak plank. That walnut floor alone, in this day, would represent a small fortune. The place was chiefly famous as possessing the only pigeon-hole table in the Eastern Illinois of that day.

Marshall was standing behind the bar when "Uncle Billy" happened in. Evidently something had gone wrong with him that day for, when "Uncle Billy" mentioned that he had come to collect for the ham, Marshall flared up and exclaimed: "Say, old man, that was the rottenest ham I ever had in my life. You don't think I am going to pay for it, do you?" Instead of argument there was action on the part of "Uncle Billy." His long right arm swung like a mill-sweep over that bar and his hand gathered in its capacious grasp coat, vest shirt, nether garment and everything in the region of the small of the back with the grip of a Cyclops. An upward heave of the arm and along came Johnnie Marshall head first over his own bar, only to be dropped face down-ward in a heap on the floor. With his foot "Uncle Billy rolled him over on his back and, looking down upon the recumbent figure with a calm, unruffled air, he remarked: "So, the ham was spiled, was it, Johnnie? Couldn't use it at all, I suppose?"

"Well, n-n-no, it wasn't exactly spiled, "Uncle Billy," replied the humbled Johnnie; and, and, uh, come to think on it, we used it all and it was pretty tolerable good." Johnny had risen to a sitting posture by this time and was further aided by Uncle Billy, who got him by the coat collar and lifted him to his feet. Still retaining his hold on the coat collar he remarked: "That 'ere ham was about as good a ham as you ever had, wasn't it, Johnnie?"

"Yes," acknowledged Johnnie, "that 'ere was a good ham; as near as I kin recollect, that was as good a ham as I ever had!" And with this acknowledgement of the excellence of the goods, Uncle Billy released his hold while Johnnie Marshall circled the end of the bar and extracted from the till one dollar and fifty cents, coin of the realm, which was the proper tariff on a fifteen-pound ham of that day at ten cents per pound and handed it over with profuse apologies for his action. Uncle Billy grimly pocketed the money and made straight for the door, and Johnnie Marshall, still rattled and flustered at the rapidity with which the events we have narrated took place, forgot to say good-by to the retreating figure, or ask him to come again.

"THE HOUSE THAT JACK BUILT"

Let us say at the outset that we are not trespassing on the domain of the ancient, well-loved nursery tales for a story. The title, however, is peculiarly applicable, since the early-day pioneers of Yellowhead so designated the habitation of a lone Pottawattomie Indian who made his home there for years. Mr. William Stratton recalls that many years ago up in Yellowhead township, a single straggler of the once numerous band of the Pottawattomi of the Prairie and the Kankakee who had formerly occupied that section, made his home on an eighty-acre "float." He was known as "Jack-Built," for short, and his place was about a mile and a half south of the Perry Stratton place, or "Yellowhead Point" where old chief Yellowhead formerly had his village.

Here he struggled manfully, though un-successfully, to adapt himself to the ways of the white man. Here he labored industriously for a time and cleared a little circular spot in the timber whereupon to raise his corn and pumpkins. Here, also, he reared a pitiful little shack whose lines followed more nearly the peculiar design of the aboriginal "tepee," even though he had at first fondly hoped to follow that of his white brother. A notable achievement of Jack's was when he planted an apple tree within the clearing in the woods. Someone, somewhere, gave him an apple tree one day and he planted it according to directions. It laid hold of the soil with its roots and grew and thrived, to Jack's great delight. Such was the response of this tree to the scant effort Jack extended that, in the course of the years it bore bountifully of an indifferent sort of fruit.

But, to Jack, this tree of the white man's was "great Medicine." When asked why he did not plant more apple trees, Indian Jack replied stolidly, "One tree make heap plenty." And the terse reply suggests one important deduction, viz: when you have enough, why worry about more. That peculiar phase of Indian philosophy which regards only today, and takes no thought of the morrow, was noticeable in all the varied activities by which Indian Jack sought to emulate the white man. There were days in the spring and early summer when his corn patch would have profited immensely had he gone into it with a hoe. The pumpkins and melons did not prosper for the same reason. When it rained, one could not be expected to do these things very well, and on those days when the sun shone high in the heavens there was the call of magnificent woodland aisles, flecked with leafy shade and sunshine, where the Great Spirit of the ancient Pottawattomi lurked and sang the old, old songs that grip one so, and beckoned, beckoned enticingly that one lone red child to throw off the self-imposed shackles of the white man and be free. Little wonder, then, that instead of tending corn he set primitive snares for the wily mink on the edge of dark pools; likewise, in the runways of the muskrat. He stalked the paths of the forest and was rewarded now and then when his ready arrow brought down a deer that still lingered in its home in the hazel copses, or a wild goose or mallard that sought the nearby water.

In the "moon of bright nights," which, in the Indian calendar is the month of April, it was then the breath of Shawandasee, "the South Wind," fell upon the woodland warm and languorous; when wild flowers opened almost over-night; when buds swelled and the sweet sap of the maple oozed from the bruised spots on their rugged trunks. And Indian Jack, sensing this quickening tide in the realm of nature sat outside his shack while the night enfolded him, and calmly and complacently he smoked, smoked the tobacco of the white man mixed with "songshasha," or dried bark of the red willow, and watched the stars and the moon and the drift of the night flights of the wild geese northward that appeared first as a small cloud and then vanished on the horizon like wisps of mist. As he sat thus, there were thoughts doubtless of the hordes of pickerel and sturgeon that, even then, were moving upstream in quest of the shallow waters of the upper swamps. The whole realm of nature was astir with its latent life and at such times Indian Jack was conscious of a feeling of peace and deep content which most surely boded ill for the crops of his little clearing in the timber. To the Indian mind the feast of good things was being spread. The season of plenty with ease was on. That charm which Indian Jack found so all-engrossing in a time like this, is, perhaps, best expressed in a bit of vagrant verse—

"In the April moonlight,
Or when frost is white
Upon the hill,
Well hunt and Well rest
When it pleases us best
Whenever we will."

Indian Jack was known to be friendly though taciturn, and frequently the boys of the neighborhood would turn out and visit him at his shack and vainly endeavor to engage him in conversation. An occasional "ugh," and a shrug was about as far as they ever got with him in the discussion of the affairs of the frontier. He made it clear, however, that he enjoyed hearing their conversation. By the older settlers of the neighborhood Jack's place was known as the "House That Jack Built." This title in time proved too unwieldly and the term "Jack Built" was substituted and meant Indian Jack or Jack's place as the case might be. For many years "Jack Built" continued to occupy his shack in the little clearing but, as the country settled up, the game grew scarcer and his interest in the little cleared patch waned almost to the point of complete extinction. If it had not been that his pioneer friends were good to him, he would have most surely suffered from hunger. There came a day at last when Jack was missed from the environs of "The House That Jack Built." Why he left after all these years of endeavor no one ever knew, for Indian Jack kept his own counsel and rarely if ever confided his plans and purposes to anyone. Quietly he found a buyer for his "float." Quietly he gathered together those few things necessary to an Indian when he takes "the long trail," after which he turned his back on "The House That Jack Built," whether with regret or not we may not say, but guiding his pony into the trail that lays towards the setting sun, he followed his people. The pioneer settlers in the town of Yellowhead, those who knew Indian Jack best, diagnosed the case as that of "Homesick Indian," and nothing more.

HOSS RACING DAYS IN OLD MOMENCE

In the old days on the Kankakee river, there wasn't a sport, a game—anything in the way of fun—that could not be found at the pioneer settlement of old Momence. Talk about your "wide-open towns"—right here is where that popular term was "coined." Many of your so-called "wide-open" towns of today are merely cheap and tawdry imitations such as would pall on the spirit of a real, dyed-in-the-wool Momence resident of sixty years ago, and give him a pain and a feeling akin to nausea. The reader should take care to remember that Momence was one of the earliest settlements on the river in Eastern Illinois. Her history harks back to the early thirties— a good ways back when one ponders on it. The Indian was here for, at that time, he had just consented to yield his domain to the "Great White Father" and, in consequence had a three-year margin under the treaty to stay or go as he chose. Apparently, he chose to stay. Mingled with these aborigines were white hunters and trappers, Frenchmen mainly, in that early day, with now and then one from down on the Wabash, in Indiana. These men who have given substance to the nation's history invested it also with an indescribable charm and color. These early-day men of the buckskin shirt and coon-skin cap, stood straight, talked straight, shot straight and, above all other things, took their whiskey straight.

Although it is generally conceded that there is nothing to be said in favor of whiskey on the whole, there is one thing to be said in favor of this old-time whiskey of the frontier, and that is, while it sometimes left its patron with a large-sized headache, it did not make him crazy altogether, as does the doubtful product of today. Among the pastimes that found favor in the eyes of this picturesque assemblage of frontier types, were the American game of poker, boxing, wrestling, foot racing and the like varied now and then by an honest-to-goodness fight. During the fifties and the sixties, with the coming of the settlers, horse-racing 'became the dominant sport, and few there were within the immediate environs of Momence who did not possess a quarter or half-mile horse. Many of these horses in the vernacular of the frontier were rated as "right likely critters." Every Saturday there was a gathering of the clans at Momence to witness some special racing event. Following this main event, generally, would occur anywhere from ten to a dozen races matched on the spur of the moment between the owners of quarter and half-mile horses, who, cheered by the sport, and keyed to the point of optimism by generous drinks of whiskey, backed their favorites with all their worldly goods. Oh, there was nothing niggardly, no note of caution in the support these old-time boys gave to the "boss" of their choice.

In that day of the late sixties, here and there a settler indulged in the luxury of a spring-seat for his lumber wagon. The spring- seat was viewed with envious eyes by those whose limited fortunes made it not only advisable but necessary to ride the "puncheon" board laid across the wagon-box. There was a lure to the spring-seat and, when the betting became brisk and spirited, a spring-seat served admirably as a final resource when the owner thereof had become reduced in ready funds. Many a spring-seat changed hands in those days on the result of a race. In consequence of this sporting proclivity on the part of early-day Momence citizens, the place was known far and wide by members of the sporting fraternity generally. For some years a gambler from the outside by the name of Manahan, made regular visits here.

His specialty was poker. Manahan was a squat, thickset individual with a benign and ingratiating personality. He wore invariably brown denim trousers, the legs of which were thrust nonchalantly into the tops of brown Morocco leather boots, a la pioneer. For many years he successfully clipped dividends from the bank rolls of unsuspecting pilgrims after the manner of his kind.

One day, it may have been round about 1870, a rather seedy looking outfit consisting of a team hitched to a light wagon, drove into Momence from the south and stopped before the old stone saloon that adjoined the Central House. Hitched to the rear of the wagon was a little bay mare. The man in charge—well, there was nothing extraordinary about him except that he was of a somewhat nervous temperament and had exceedingly sharp, gray eyes, deep set and obscured by heavy, bushy eyebrows. He made his way into the bar and called for whiskey in rather an ostentatious manner. He not only called for one but several whiskies within the space of a few minutes, during which he made it known by way of a general statement to that effect, that he had a "hoss" that could do a quarter-mile so neatly and handily that he made most of his competitors look like they were anchored to the ground.

Of course, the crowd was interested on the instant, and of course, there were those who recalled that citizen Jake Hess owned what was conceded to be, the best quarter- "hoss" in all the country round about. Amid a good deal of stir and excitement, Hess was sent for, and, on his arrival, the crowd and the stranger moved out to where the team was standing and there, in the harness, stood a little roan horse with harness marks deeply cut into the hair of neck and shoulders and sides. This animal, the stranger stoutly affirmed, could beat anything they had in a quarter-mile go, at least he had $250 that said so. Hess hurriedly took in the animal with his practiced eye, and then as hurriedly matched the stranger for $250 a side. There was a perfect hubbub of excitement as the crowd moved on to the west side of town to that main east and west road which, for years had served as a track for these impromptu equine events. Arriving at the place the stranger peeled the harness from the roan horse and then announced that he would ride the animal himself, much to the surprise of the crowd. After some preliminary scoring the horses got away down the stretch, and, almost from the first the Hess mare ran away from her adversary. It was a pretty bad defeat; even the stranger was obliged to admit that.

There was great rejoicing, however, among the native population of Momence, whose sporting traditions thus remained unimpaired, and on the return of the crowd to town they sought out the old stone saloon, there to talk it over and drink a bumper or two to the health of the Hess mare meanwhile. The stranger accompanied them. Apparently he was a good loser—one who was game all the way through. As he stood at the bar with Hess he talked volubly and paid a handsome tribute to the performance of the Hess mare. "Why," said he, as he put down the glass, "that hoss of yourn got up and humped himself jest like a skeered ghost ahead of a streak of double-geared lightnin'! I ain't never been so beat in sizin' up a hoss in all my life! You won all right, mister—you won!" There was another round of drinks. The crowd found the situation much to their liking. The owner of the victorious horse felt a delightful glow that had the effect of deepening the pink in his cheeks and caused the moisture to stand out comfortably on his forehead. He was conscious, also, of an increasing chest expansion as the merits of his horse were so generously acknowledged by the vanquished.

Altogether the situation was opportune, auspicious, although with our deeper knowledge of the mysteries of psycho analysis, it would have been spoken of in this day as the "psychological moment," one that a person with dark, ulterior motives, would have seized upon quickly and with confidence. That the stranger was an adept in sizing up just such situations there can be no doubt. Very much to the surprise of everyone present, he proposed another trial of speed with the Hess mare and the little bay mare that followed demurely at the tail of the wagon. "I'll lay five hundred on her," said he, "with just one condition, and that is that she be permitted to run the heat without any rider whatever!" The crowd gasped. Could he mean it? Surely the whiskey he had partaken of had gone to his head! Hess snapped at the offer amid the applause and congratulations of the onlookers. The money was put up, and again the crowd repaired to the track west of town. There is a different tale we have to tell concerning this second trial of speed. It is a tale in which there is no element of joy or pleasure for such as risked their money on the local horse. There were things that took place at that second race of which the sober second-thought and judgment of the crowd took no note until long after it was too late. Most notable among the things that happened— that incident which, perhaps, was most significant of disaster—was when a stranger mounted to the top of the nearby "stake-and rider fence" and, opening a large leather bag, containing money, announced that he was then and there prepared to lay any amount on the riderless horse. Even then the crowd asked no questions but surged about the mysterious stranger as he stood on his precarious perch, and registered many a bet of five or ten or twenty, and not a few larger amounts than that. Our informant, as he pictured the scene in his mind's eye, remarked: "I kin see 'im yet" Hence you may know, dear reader, that this individual was a real entity and not a fabrication.

The horses, for some time in readiness for the race, were held in abeyance until the betting populace had been duly accommodated.

As for the race itself, there is not much to be said. It was short, sharp and decisive—especially the latter. The demure, docile little mare that followed the tail-end of the wagon, meek and lamb-like, was a whirlwind. Nothing less would have done her justice. She crossed the mark lengths ahead of the Hess mare and, at a word from her master, slowed down and turned and trotted up to him, and then the crowd knew that she had been trained to the business. And by that sign, too, they also realized that they had been most artistically "flim-flammed."

There was a good deal of liquor consumed by that crowd on their return to the old stone saloon. Tradition has it that each fellow bought his own. Those who could not buy, "stood-off" the bar-tender. They who could neither "buy" nor "stand-off" the "barkeeper," endured the pangs of pitiless drought amid a gloom which resembled that in "Mudd-ville," after "the mighty Casey had struck out." Tradition further insists that this was the most complete and artistic "skinning" ever perpetrated on a sporting community in all the history of Kankakee county. Days after it was recalled that the man with the seedy looking outfit and the mysterious stranger with the bag full of money worked with feverish haste, and within a few minutes after the race were hitting the highway north out of town. The last ever seen of the seedy looking outfit it was still moving north over the highway and, lo and behold, there sat in the seat with the driver, the now familiar form of the erstwhile mysterious stranger, holding on his knees and hugging closely an old leather bag whose sides bulged with a goodly quantity of Momence "Kale." And, apparently, these two were not strangers.

THE LAST ENCAMPMENT OF THE INDIANS

The Hon. Clark Brown, of Union, Missouri, a member of the Missouri legislature, formerly a resident of Momence, has shown his deep interest and appreciation of the work undertaken by the writer to preserve that which is worthwhile in the lives of the early day settlers, by furnishing us the following incident

"The greatest return of the children of the prairies to a last view of their old hunting grounds, was when the report came, in the summer of 1853, that a tribe of Indians had come back and encamped in Bourbonnais Grove.

Quite a company from our neighborhood, east of the grove, decided to go down and see the Indians. Some went in buggies, and some on horseback, and the seeing was well worth the going. On a platform of light poles two feet above the ground in an open spot in LeVasseur's sugar grove, the old chief and his squaw were squatted amid their blankets and other belongings. I remember that "Injun" as the largest squab of human flesh and fat I ever saw. His weight must have been four hundred pounds or more. We saw no efforts upon his part to stand on his feet that day. His clothing consisted of one garment, a large sheet of canvas, seemingly, which buttoned about his neck, enveloping him in its ample folds. It might have been considered the original of the "Mother Hubbard."

The old couple seemed to take much pride in each other, she taking pains with the little rat-tail braids with a few strands of white hair mixed with his black hair that hung from the eaves of his formidable head. Both chattered or grunted freely with the company which paid them the most attention during the day. The rest of the thirty or forty members of the tribe were in tepees, or brush wigwams, arranged in a circle at some distance from their chief. But little shelter was required in a summer encampment.

Their toilet was lacking altogether in style. All efforts at clothing were a conglomerate mixture—no two alike—of white man's and aboriginal dress. One article, the blanket, prevailed quite generally with the women. But there was a variety of styles when it came to wearing them. With some the blanket would be suspended from the loins, while others spread it over their shoulders. The splitskirt had not then come into style, and their blankets were not sufficiently ample in dimensions to permit of much of a "split."

Apparently, the girls as they approached the stage of womanhood, had their hair plaited into one long braid, and with many, this braid was, at regular intervals of several inches, pounded full of mud or moist clay which dried and staid hard. This not only held the hair from coming down but was an aid to ornamentation, feathers and beads being lavishly used. One thing that spoke well for the tribe, there were no evidences of cross-breeding. All had the same degree of "smoked bacon" complexion, the same coarse, black hair.

Not many of the tribe, between the old chief and the children and youths with their bows and arrows with which they shot the big copper pennies from a split stick set in the ground, seemed desirous of cultivating the acquaintance of the visitors. No doubt they all could make use of our language if they had so desired, but they seemed not inclined to discuss the latest fashions nor disposed to relate the neighborhood gossip, even if such things are the admitted prerogative of "the female of the species."

There were other echoes also from the west side of the great river. Momence, like a few others, had selected a reservation, and seemingly with very good judgment. Momence, it should be borne in mind, was an Indian chief. We might say it consisted of a piece of the Kankakee river embracing the island, on which was once a grist mill, and quite an extent of shore on either side of the river. By this time, no doubt, the whole site is occupied by the city of Momence. The writer once had the pleasure of an interview during a railroad ride with this original proprietor. He was a large, well-proportioned Indian, dressed in white man's fashion. This was his last visit to his old range on the Kankakee. Probably, Indian-like, he had been accused of selling his reservation to two parties. We never heard how the courts decided the ownership."

MOMENCE INCORPORATES

Momence took steps to incorporate as a village nearly three-quarters of a century ago. At that time the little settlement of the river had near unto two hundred souls, five or six stores and several small industries. The truth is, Momence was a smug, tight little border settlement of substance while Kankakee was still an infant in swaddling clothes, "mewling and spewing in its nurse's arms." There are no records extant relating to this momentous event, sad to say. The memory of the old-time pioneer holds all there is to be said about it. It is generally conceded that the effort to incorporate took place about the year 1853, some time after the election held to locate the county-seat of the newly organized county of Kankakee, the disastrous outcome of which, disappointing to the hopes and ambitions of Momence, has been set forth in a previous volume of stories of early days. Momence as a "border town" retained her chief characteristics in this respect for many a year. Her people, originally, were the real, dyed-in-the-wool frontier type, and were restless and sensitive to a degree of restraints imposed by law or the customs of civilization.

These old-town men were positive giants! Scarcely a man of them measured less than six feet, and many of them were taller than that! Naturally they were possessed of a grit and a brawn that made them formidable in case of personal encounter.

The life of the old town of the border was one of internecine strife in a day when a mere difference of opinion, if nothing more, sufficed to start hostilities. Bill Graham and Dan Parmlee, two backwoods giants fell out one day and in the fight that ensued, Graham seized a neck-yoke that chanced to be lying close by and nearly brained his adversary with it. That old Dan lived at all, after this savage onslaught, was one of the wonders. But frontier skulls were made to stand hard knocks. For months afterwards, when Parmlee came to town, it was noticed that he did not bring his rifle with him. It seemed strange for the two were inseparable, ordinarily. Asked one day about it and why he did not carry it as of yore, old Dan replied in his char-acteristic way: "Wal, it's like this; if I had that thar rifle with me and happened to run across Bill Graham at the same time, by God I'd kill 'im! Yes I would—sure as Adam and Eve lived in the Garden of Eden. Me and Bill used to be purty good friends, and he ain't such a bad feller anyway. Mebbe if I'd got hold of that neck-yoke fust—well, anyway I leave the old rifle home so's old Dan won't do anything hasty, besides, old Dan's purty good yit, if wust comes to wust!"

It was always a sport-loving community, this little, backwoods settlement of the Kankakee, whose people, of the stature and endowed with the brawn of giants, instead of being occupied with the more serious things of life, leaned rather to the sports and games and trifling things which made up, in large part, the life of wilderness days. Envy and avarice had not laid hold of the hearts and consciences of these people in that day. It was a generation born to the corn-pone and the hickory shirt, in which no element of superiority of race or breeding was acknowledged except the superiority of physical force. The "best man" in every community held his head high. He had a right to, for his quality had been subjected to the acid test of many and many a battle. The marshmen and the woodsmen, and the men of the river and the prairies all loved to congregate at Momence, for there their fun-loving natures always found that which was a joy to the soul.

Every other man, in that day, had a "race-hoss," and over on the western edge of town, just opposite the present city limits, was the track over which they ran. Here, in the heat of excitement, a man often bet everything he had in the world, even to the buckskin shirt on his back or the more treasured "spring-seat," that later graced the lumber- wagon and bespoke a prosperity quite in advance of the generality of frontier folk. After the "hoss-race" there would be foot-races, a wrestling match, a boxing bout or two, a cock-fight— anything—even a dog fight. And, at the bare mention of dogs, the pioneer memory recalls that, on one memorable occasion, two perfectly staid and well-behaved hounds of the "lop-eared" species, followed their respective masters to the festivities held in old Momence and, becoming imbued with the spirit and enthusiasm of the times, lit into one another in a regular rough-and-tumble fight. The crowd was interested and bet liberally on the outcome of the fight. All might have been well and the "finger that writes," might have remained inert and motionless had not one of the men whose dog was getting somewhat the worst of the battle, kicked the op-posing dog heavily in the jowl. As a result of this impulsive, ill-considered act, there ensued a fight instanter between the respective owners of the dogs, and, if the pioneer memory may be relied upon, "it was a scrap worth going miles to see."

Not only that; for a time there was imminent danger that the whole masculine population was going to become involved, for each man had his friends and the spirit of fair-play and partisan rivalry ruled a formidable factor in the affairs of men of the border. The frontiersman who thus so whole-heartedly upheld the rights and reputation of his dog was about six feet four in his stockings. After severely chastising his adversary, he pushed his way into the backwoods saloon followed by an admiring flock of partisans and, as he leaned upon the bar, he murmured to the bar-tender: "Gimme a drink! It tires me to fight!"

That which we have related in the foregoing is necessary if one is to understand and fully appreciate the spirit and temper of a people who, confronted by a proposition to incorporate as a village, found themselves unable to agree, with any sort of unanimity, as to the benefits of such incorporation. Most of them felt that it meant a surrender of individual rights such as they had enjoyed in the past, a curtailing of the old, wide-open, free-and-easy life which was so greatly enjoyed when the habitues of the river and woods and prairies took a day off. "Give me liberty, or give me death," is a slogan which first had its inception in the hearts and minds of just such men as these. We are told that the first fight over the proposition to incorporate took place in 1853, and that it was a fight sure enough. There were hatreds engendered at that time that lived and smouldered and flared forth now and then for many and many a year. After the lapse of nearly seventy-five years the high-lights and salient points of this particular picture of border days have faded into nothingness. The fight was a bitter one, it is true, but one can scarcely get head or tail of it. In some quarters it is said that it was a conflict of "the new comers" against the old-timers," a conflict of "new ideas" against "old," an arraying of the growing church element against these primitive types of the border, in order to control them, if only in a small way, and restrain the wild and hilarious spirit that so readily manifested itself whenever they met. Elder Burr, the circuit rider, was prominently identified as a leader of the forces for incorporation. He was threatened, secretly and openly, by the more headstrong of the opposing side. But he went his way, calm, imperturable, temperate of manner in his support of the incorporation project, yet firm and unyielding as a rock in his purpose.

As a result of this early-day battle of the ballots in old Momence, the proposition to in-corporate won by a small vote, surprising as it may seem. There were hatreds and personal dislikes and jealousies that registered in this first election. The result was hardly a genuine reflex of the real, underlying sentiment in the minds of the voters. They had "got even" with someone, that's all. Momence set out uncertainly upon the new municipal life called for by ordinances and state laws. The very first levying of a corporation tax occasioned a roar of protest on the part of both the "fors" and "against." With the issuance of the decree of "poll-tax" on every male head of voting age within the corporation, there came positive rebellion. They would not pay three dollars, neither would they work in lieu of not paying, upon the streets of the village. On this they were united —unanimous—for once in their lives. Our friends who had supported so whole-heartedly this move towards civilization were as unruly, as boisterous and rantankerous as a two-year old Texas steer when he first feels the rope tighten on his neck. The newly elected officers, swelled with a proper sense of their importance and the dignity of office, on finding their orders disregarded by the populace, proceeded to make an example of some of the more prominent of the objectors and, in effect, undertook to "hog-tie" and "brand" them as undesirable citizens. The majesty of the newborn authority of statutes and ordinances was invoked and the recalcitrants were properly sued and properly found guilty of a disregard for the mandates of the law as administered by its officers.

Though they were found guilty they would not pay, and the remaining alternative, that of working, they spurned as something beneath the consideration of freemen. By this act they added to the sum total of their delinquencies that of lese-majeste, which is most serious indeed, except in cases where frontiersmen are concerned. The municipality, at that time, had not achieved financial prosperity sufficient to enable it to have a calaboose, and the village marshal would have as quickly considered suicide as he would an order to arrest and incarcerate these border men who resented corporate encroachment on their personal liberties. In the end, several of these cases were appealed to higher courts, and there, apparently, the matter dropped. Under such discouraging circumstances was organized law ushered into the old river settlement of Momence. This substitution of the new order for the old lived but a day, and then slowly but surely withered and faded away completely, so that for several years following this attempt at incorporation, the place knew no other law but that of the border—force. It was not until the late fifties that incorporation became a recognized fact, and round about 1860, when the trustees put into effect an ordinance restraining the cows of the villagers from running at large, it was then that citizen Peter Terrill was mov-ed to observe to Justice M. 0. Clark: "It do beat all how there's always more damn fools than smart men!"

This is a photographic reproduction of a section of a famous coverlet of Pioneer days. Made by Mrs. Maria Gundy Nichols, wife of William Nichols, one of the earliest pioneers. It is an intricate "two-color" design and a work of art. It was made on what was knowns as a "double loom." Situated in a log cabin across the road from the present home of Mrs. Malinda Nichols, northeast of Momence. The pattern is white and blue, and Mrs. Marcia Nichols carded spun and colored the woo. Used in weaving, it was made some year prior to her death which occurred in 1838

AN ANCIENT HUNTING GROUND

I.

Momence, as a frontier town, was most happily situated on the outskirts of one of the finest hunting grounds in all the middle west—famous Beaver Lake. If we are to believe fully the testimony of men who lived here and hunted and trapped and fished in primeval days, before the destructive blight of so-called civilization had fallen upon the land, the great marshes of the Kankakee surpassed in extent and prodigal abundance any other spot in the United States. Where the Kankakee emerges from across the state-line of Indiana into Illinois, after miles on miles of tortuous turnings and twistings, it pauses for a space and disposes its flood in quiet labyrinthine channels among islands, overflowing into shady nooks and shallow bayous and marshes.

Seventy-five years ago these islands were heavily timbered as was, also, much of the adjacent high ground. Fortunately much of this timber still remains to delight the eye. Here may be found giant patriarchs grimly holding their ground—oaks, walnuts, glorious elms and the stately sycamore. In this day of the Indiana, has suffered irreparable injury of late years on account of an ambitious reclamation project which,' seeks to divert the waters of the Kankakee from their old bed into deeper and straighter channels. There are places where the bed of the old stream is isolated—cut-off entirely from the original stream by huge ditches, staring, ugly, straight as a plummet-line.

The shades of LaSalle and Tonty would exclaim with righteous indignation at the transformation which this ancient stream has undergone of late, the stream which they first knew as the "Theak-ki-ki," beautiful, winding, picturesque in the extreme.

There is no more beautiful stretch of river in the entire course of the Kankakee than that which lies between Momence and the Indiana state-line. It is native wilderness conveniently near yet, in a sense, removed from the centers of population. Deep in its shadows the trapper still lingers, and the pale blue wood smoke which rises here and there above the fringe of timber, proclaims the summer home of the habitant with a taint of the primeval in his blood. These sheltered places still harbor the red-bird, the blue-bird, the thrush and various other of nature's songsters who thrill the heart of the wayfarer with a flash of dazzling color, and delight the ear with song unchanged and unchanging with the years from the earliest day when creation dawned. These places are still haunted in numbers by the shrewd, lazy, lumbering crow, who, from sheer deviltry, preys upon the farmer and thus provokes his ire, when he could just as easily get his living in the woods. Here the blackbird hosts seem undiminished. The wild, sweet note of Bob-White, heard once in this wilderness paradise of the upper Kankakee, will haunt one to the end of his days. The wood-ducks, the mallards, the pin-tails and blue-bills as though mindful of traditions of the long ago, still patronize these charming nooks on the Kankakee between Momence and the state-line, not in numbers, it is true, but enough so to give an air of realism to the ancient habitat that was.

Vandalism stops short at the Illinois-Indiana state-line. Here the Kankakee pursues its accustomed course, wandering aimlessly and unrestrained as befits a strong traditionally beautified historic.

There is a fox taken now and then, a mink, a skunk, a family of raccoons. How these dwellers of the wild do cling to their own! From the deepest and darkest of these sylvan retreats a wolf comes forth stealthily, even in this day, and raids a neighboring hen-house, notwithstanding there is a price on his head. And, when he falls at last before the dogs of the white man, he loses his scalp but gets from three to six lines solid in the local paper. He is a member of society more dreaded than the "bootlegger," hence his taking off is worthy of notice.

In this nook of remaining wilderness above Momence, wherever the shallow waters of the Kankakee reach landward and form a bayou there, in numbers, appears the quaint homes of the musk-rats, built in the shape, in the same manner, and of the same materials as were used yesterday— (two hundred years ago, when the French came down the river), or let us say, last week, (a thousand years ago), which amounts to the same thing in the chronology of the patient, plodding rats. Do we weary you with these small details of the river wilderness? We hope not. Only mankind is fickle and unstable and changing in his moods. The dwellers of the wild, through instinct, follow an unvarying plan of doing things. They rarely or never deviate from it. Perhaps you have not been impressed by the fact that, from the earliest days, the skin of the musk-rat has had a commercial value, varying of course, with the times. In 1849 the trapper would call for a drink of whiskey over the backwoods bar at Momence, and throw down a rat hide in payment therefor. "The musk-rat hide was the "small change" of the frontier for many and many a year. During the late war the price of a prime, dark musk-rat skin was six to seven dollars. We tell you upon the authority of a "shantyman" of the Kankakee whose word we respect, that the finest of all muskrat skins used for milady's coat, those skins which are dark and glossy and thick, and which bespeak elegance, come mainly from the bayous and ditches of the great swamp region of the Kankakee. It pays sometimes to cultivate your next-door neighbor. He may not prove to be a college-bred man, but he is wise to the little things of the realm in which he lives, the possessor of a degree in that great university of the out of doors.

There are huts, habitations of mankind, set in this charming bit of up-river wilderness of today and well-worn paths lead to them and away until they lose themselves in interminable turnings and twistings. These paths, more ancient still than anything the wilderness holds except the river itself, were made by the feet of the Pottawattomi dwellers long ago. The man of the city presses relentlessly upon the outskirts of this wild domain with his summer home so that the man of the hut, appalled at the thought of fraternizing with affluence and luxury, shrinks more deeply into the shadow of the sheltered spots and turns his back upon it all. You say he is peculiar? Well, perhaps so. But, one must remember, there is a "kick-back," as they used to say in old times, when alluding to a man's ancestral lines—a "kick-back" to sires who lived by the open fire, out under the stars, and who fraternized with the Pottawattomi and nature. These later-day huts lean noticeably and the boards are weathered and gray. Within, one will find the stub of a candle or a kerosene lamp instead of an electric bulb. The library is a newspaper, days old. There is a small, rusty stove, a limited array of dented tinware—a piece or two of crockery, much chipped.

A TYPICAL TRAPPER'S CABIN

It Leans a Little, and its Boards are Weathered and Gray, but, if it Lacks in Luxury, it has Peace and Quiet and Deep Content.

There is a breech- loading gun and accoutrements, traps, and fishing paraphernalia in abundance. This habitant of the silent places is not much concerned in business, political parties and policies, or education. That function which would be most likely to enlist his presence and insure his staying up late at night, would be a poker party. Generally, he stalls not at a glass of whiskey. His most intimate personal accompaniments are a strong, black pipe and a hound dog or two with lopping ears, wise as their master. In this day he foregoes the picturesque garb of the hunter and trapper for he has outlived the days of buckskin, which was the fabric of the frontier, and cotton textiles are abundant and cheap. In this bit of virgin wild of the Kankakee he lingers for a space, the only connecting link between the simple life of the old frontier and the flaming, heedless, headlong luxury of the great twentieth century. In another generation he, too, will have passed, and among the thousands who follow there will not be one to take his place—the life is too slow!

II.

Above Momence a little way the Kankakee, as if conscious that the swamps and bayous and gleaming yellow sands have been left behind, gathers her tide serenely between high banks and swings away to the southwest in long, graceful, sinuous curves, broadening perceptibly and growing in beauty and majesty at every mile as she hurries through the beautiful vale of the Kankakee to her meeting with the DesPlaines. The swamps and bayous between Momence and the Indiana state-line are but the beginnings of the "Great Kankakee Marsh/" whose huge dimensions numbering thousands upon thousands of acres, overspread mile on mile of Indiana territory north and south of the river and east of the Indiana line. There were vast open stretches of water set with oak-crowned is-lands, thousands of acres of shallow marsh grown up to cattails, wild rice and rushes, the nesting ground of the wild, migratory hordes of the upper air. From time immemorial this was a famous hunting ground for the Miamis, the Wyandottes, the Illinois, and more particularly the Pottawattomi of the Prairie and the Kankakee, whose domain it came at last to be. Abundant evidences of Indian occupation are still found in this day where the winds, in their play, make eddies in the sands of the ridges about the old lake bed, revealing an ancient arrow-head, or stone axe or other trophy which the practiced eye of the modern collector seizes upon and bears away in triumph.

Mr. Edward Hamilton, of Morocco, Indiana, after fifty years devoted to this interesting pursuit, has acquired a most valuable and interesting collection of flint and stone implements, indispensable to aboriginal life. The collection contains about everything of which the Indian made use in his daily life. Among the hundreds of arrow-heads, awls, drills, mortars, skinning tools, banner-stones and ceremonial stones contained in this collection, the smaller "bird-points," three-quarters of an inch in length, exquisitely fashioned, more often moves the visitor to delighted exclamation. That these pieces were patiently chipped by the native workman by means of the notched flint seems at first impossible. Whatever the means he employed the ancient arrow-maker was a master craftsman who carried the secrets of his art with him when he passed. These pieces which the sands reveal to us in this day are memorials of an era when the Indian reigned supreme in the great swamp region.

When, and by whom, were these retreats of "Big Bogus," "Little Bogus" and the Beaver Lake country generally, discovered and made use of? That is a query which, in all probability, will forever remain unanswered. LaSalle's men, as early as 1679, must have availed themselves of the plenty abounding there, even though it was late December when he made his memorable trip down the Kankakee.

Father Hennepin recorded the fact that his Mohican hunters were abroad, that LaSalle himself got lost in the oak scrub and sand- dunes, and that somewhere, southwest of the portage, they ran across a buffalo bull hopelessly mired in the river muck. The nearest approach to a fixed date when a white man hunted in the Beaver Lake region, is that mentioned by the famous pioneer trader, Gur- don S. Hubbard, in his memoirs—March 1827. Long before that day, however, the French voyageur and coureur de bois hunted and trapped and fished the Kankakee and its marsh environs, but these men left no written record of their comings and goings. They were frontiersmen—not writers.

There was a section of the Kankakee where the river writhed and twisted and turned back upon itself in a series of startling zigzag movements as a result of the uncertain meanderings of the ancient ice-cap, which moved ever so slowly and ploughed a channel for the stream—a nook of twisting river and shallow swamps, lying to the south-east of DeMotte, Indiana, and extending to the state-line, which was as sweet a paradise for the hunter and trapper as ever existed anywhere under the sun. In this bit of river country, east from Shelby, Indiana, there was first, "Bumbaloo," the wilderness home of that sturdy Canadian, "Hank" Granger; then Little Hickory, Red Oak, Indian Garden, (which must not be confused with

Indian Garden located above Momence), Jerry's Island (named after old Jerry Kinney), Beech Ridge, French Island, and Grape Island. In this day a perfectly new river channel operates from a point or bend in the Kankakee above Grape Island in an air line to the state-line, and the ancient river bed, thus cut off, is now grown up to saw-grass, cat-tails and rushes, with now and then a stagnant pool, covered with green scum. Here in this once delightful nook of the Kankakee, such men as Folsom, Brainerd, Ritter, Granger, Seymour, Summers, Duesenberg, Sweeney, Bissell, Goodrich, Broady and Irvin, old-timers with a reputation both sides of the state-line, carried on for years.

Returning to Gurdon S. Hubbard, the trader, an unusual experience incident to the trip of March 1827 to Beaver Lake, is of interest, and we reproduce it.

"One cold March day in 1827, I went to the Beaver Creek Lake for a hunt. This was a part of the great Kankakee Marsh, and geese and ducks and swan were very abundant. The fall previous I had hidden a canoe in the vicinity of the lake and about thirteen miles from my trading house, and this I found with little difficulty. I hunted until nearly dark, when, thinking it was too dark to return home, I camped for the night on a small island in the lake. There were no trees, but I made a fire of driftwood, and having cooked some game for my supper, lay down and soon fell asleep. Sometime in the night I awoke in great pain, and found that my fire had nearly burned out. I managed to replenish it, but the pain continued, being most severe in my legs, and by morning it increased to such an extent that I could not reach the canoe

.

EAST FROM THE STATE-LINE IN INDIANA

Here the Kankakee Appears in a new Channel cut Straight as a Line from the State-line as far as Grape Island, Miles Away to the East. Miles on Miles of Ancient River bed Have Been Thus cut off From the Stream.

About ten o'clock an Indian came down to the lake and I called to him and told him of my condition, and with his assistance reached the canoe, and finally the main shore. I sent the Indian to Iroquois (Bunkum), with orders for my men to come and bring with them a horse and harness. On their arrival I had the horse hitched to the canoe and myself placed therein, and started in this manner to ride home. I soon found that I could not stand the jarring of the canoe as it was drawn over the rough ground, and halted until some better means of travel could be devised.

I sent back to Iroquois for two more men, which necessitated my camping for one night more. On their arrival they constructed, with poles and blankets, a litter upon which they bore me safely and quite comfortably home. I had a severe attack of inflammatory rheumatism, which confined me to the house for three or four weeks, and from which I did not fully recover for eighteen months. I doctored myself with poultices of elm and decoctions of various herbs."

III.

During the old days of the border and later, on the advent of spring when the myriad hosts of the air, ducks, geese, brant, crane, swan and blue heron poured in untold numbers into this natural haven of the wild, it was then that the youth and middle-aged of the little settlement of Momence, on the river, were stirred to feverish activity and prepared for a campaign of slaughter. Their numbers were increased by hunters from the countryside and from far and near, for the season of sport and plenty was on. For the hunters of the Illinois country and beyond, Momence was the gateway.

But, before the Promised Land of this great game retreat could be reached, however, the awful mud of "Lynd's Lane" had to be negotiated. "Lynd's Lane" originates near the Lorain School south of the river and, for years, has been the chief artery of travel to the east and the Beaver Lake country. This road of late years has been robbed of most of its terrors by reason of having been drained and built up of stone. "Lynd's Lane" in the days of the frontier, however, was a meandering trail south of the river that wound its way uncertainly to the east among quagmires, islands of bulrushes and "elbow brush," across boggy, springy stretches of quaking marsh up to the near vicinity of the Tiffany Brick Works of today, where Dr. Lynds formerly had his home. The swamp in its entirety is known as "Hess' Slough." This lane, then, in reality "Dr. Lynd's Lane," by a peculiar colloquial lapse on the part of Momence citizens, is called by every mother's son of them "Lyon's Lane."

At most times of the year but more particularly in the spring and fall, it was a bottomless morass of sticky, clinging mud. It was the bete noir of the traveler and the hunter by whom it was tacitly admitted that it possessed all the qualities claimed by a certain darkey for his coon-trap, viz: "If hit doan git 'em a-comin', hit sure will git 'em when dey's a-gwine!" Ah, many a hunter caught in its treacherous depths has made known to a waiting world in language vigorous, profane, picturesque, that "cornin' or gwine," it was all the same to "Lyon's Lane." Many a rig stuck in its tenacious depths had to be lightened of its load before a wheel could turn.

Many a returning hunter found it necessary to sacrifice the greater part of his kill to the insatiable maw of "Lyon's Lane." The terrors of "Lyon's Lane," in time, were not only anathamatized in good, old-fashioned orthodox style, but apostrophized, as the following quatrain of frontier origin will show:

"There is a place called 'Lyon's Lane,'
That/'s always filled with mud;
And hunters plunged beneath that flood,
Lose all their ducks and game!"

Scattered throughout this wide country of ours, in almost every state in the Union, are old, gray-haired men who, at some time in their youth, braved the mud of "Lyon's Lane," the rain and sleet and snows of early March, to lay in a "blind" made of "cat-tails," wild rice and rushes piled high in the lee of a convenient musk-rat house in the "Black Marsh," and took toll of the wild horde as it came tumbling in. Blessed is he who lived in those primitive days. For all such there is an inheritance of stirring memories that thrills the blood and quickens the pulse.

How is one to go about it to tell the interesting story of this moving picture of wild life of the long ago? As Judge Hunter says: "Man! Man! Man! The spectacle was too stupendous for words! He would have to have known something of those days; he should have lived in the swamps as I did, weeks and months at a time; he would have to have the echo of the deafening clamor of all this wild life in his ears and sense the beating of thousands of wings in the air and envision the gray-white bodies and yellow legs of these mighty hosts all set to drop into the open water spaces among the rushes and wild rice! A man who seeks to understand it all should have, at some time in his life, experienced that mighty thrill of elation that comes to the hunter when, at the crack of his gun, not one but half a dozen, maybe a dozen fine birds came tumbling down into the water! A man would have to know all that means and more—and then he could not make novice understand."

Often in the fall of the year, the marsh would be burned over, at least sections of it would be, but it never burned cleanly. Here and there would be left islands of rushes, saw-grass, cat-tails and other swamp growth, in the center of which was generally to be found a musk-rat house or two. The hunter would push his boat into a standing mass like this and, where there happened to be a musk-rat house, he would kick a trench through the top of it and run his boat therein. He would then tear out the top of an adjoining muskrat habitation in which to accommodate his dogs and the game as fast as they brought it in. A good retriever in that day surely earned his board and keep. A hunter with a good dog never paid any attention to the game as it fell to his gun. It was the dog's business to bring it in, and he was faithful to the job. When the shooting was brisk he was in the ice-cold water for hours at a time, and when the wind blew cold so that the spray froze on the sides of the boat, icicles hung like pendants from the dog's shaggy coat, and tinkled like castanets. At the camp a cosy box of straw awaited him nearby the stove and, after a generous feed of coarse cornmeal mush, he turned in and immediately forgot the trials and hardships of the day.

THE SITE OF HUBBARD'S TRADING POST

There was a Time When the Life of the Wilderness Revolved Around This Spot. Here Gurdon S. Hubbard had his Trading Post on the Iroquois as early as 1828. The old "Trail" Marks are Still Visible Nearby but Everything Else has Vanished.

79

In the spring the fly-way was from the southwest to the northeast. At this time small, red-head teal occupied these waters literally by the hundreds of thousands. Out on the broad expanse of the lake proper and the open reaches of that famous hunting ground known as the "Gaff Ranch," there dwelt the mallards, geese and swan literally by the acre. Judge Hunter recalls that often as he laid in his "blind he has watched a flight of these red-heads go over, scarcely six feet above his head, a veritable cloud of them acres in extent, a living blanket four or five feet in thickness as it seemed. How they can fly in such numbers and not interfere with one another is one of the secrets of wild life known only to the habitants of the wild. These birds were small and seldom shot at for the reason that the real hunter disdained to waste his powder and shot on them, but waited for the mallard, pin-tail, geese and swan—something worthwhile. Decoys were plentifully used in the old days, and long before the day of the "duck-callers" or "squawkers," there were many hunters who could successfully lure the mallards and pin-tails to circle over them. Walter Hobbie could imitate the "honk" of a goose with that high-pitched nasal twang of his so that a bird within earshot would stop, look and listen. Frank Longpre of Momence, however, in his palmy days, could just naturally make a goose get down among the rushes and look for him, his wild, strident "honk" sounding for all the world like "Whar are yuh! Whar are yuh! Whar are yuh!"

Joseph Kite, a nearby resident of Lake Village, Indiana, a member of the well-remembered Kite Brothers' hunting organization of the early days, became thoughtful and reminiscent when approached on the question Beaver Lake's glorious days of plenty.

Cold, hard figures, even though one employs the term thousands, or hundreds of thousands, fail to adequately express the idea of unlimited numbers of wild fowl that occupied the waters of the lake and the adjacent nesting grounds of the marshes, in the opinion of Mr. Kite. Beaver Lake contained, roughly speaking, thirty-five to forty thousand acres, mostly covered with water. Therefore, he would use the term "acres," as most expressive of numbers of the mallards, geese, brant, and swan that frequented the place. The swan especially were numerous. He has stood in the door of his shack on Johnson Island and shot them. He and his brothers brought in one day a top-box wagon load of these birds. They used to ship them to Chicago. Sometimes they would get one dollar apiece for swan that weighed from seventeen to twenty pounds. More often they got less, and not infrequently it happened that the commission man forgot them entirely. The wagon load of swan mentioned they did not ship but skinned the carcasses and tacked them up on the walls of their shack to dry. These skins had a commercial value over and above the meat, which was excellent. The feathers of pure white were valuable, and after they were extracted there was left the beautiful, soft, white down which, in the early days, constituted the genuine "swan's-down," so much esteemed for the trimming of ladies' garments. Their efforts in this instance, however, met with disaster. The moths got into them and ruined the entire lot.

There was an element of the spectacular and the beautiful in this moving picture of the wild life of the lake, especially at such times when the swan rose in numbers from the surface of the water, a roaring, turbulent, billowy mass, their white breasts and wings glowing with an irridescence like mother of pearl where the sunlight was reflected from them. At other times they would come head- on into the wind, twisting, rolling like a milk- white cloud.

Victor Brassard, of Momence, as a youth hunted with his father in the days of Beaver Lake's plenty. His observations are interesting. Often, he says, ducks and geese were slaughtered by the thousands merely for their feathers, for, in that day of the frontier, every well-ordered household had feather beds, since replaced by the more modern mattress. There was always a market for the feathers and fairly good prices the rule. Heavy birds like geese and swan, on rising make a run head on into the wind. The airplane of today employs much the same tactics to insure a successful get-away. Sometimes numbers of these birds would be stampeded into attempting flight before they had a chance to acquire momentum by running into the wind, and the result was always a squawking, dis-organized, helter-skelter mass, helpless before the guns of the hunters.

The flight of these vast hordes in their fall migration to the south was an interesting and impressive spectacle. One could count upon its taking place anywhere from the 20th to the 31st of October and rarely miss it. The "swamp-rat," wise to every sound and movement of the wild seemed to be able to forecast their departure with a degree of success that was little short of uncanny. For several days prior to this great event, ducks and geese would gather in the open spaces of water, a huge convention considering a weighty enterprise. Ever and anon there would be a terrific upheaval in the mass and thousands of them would take wing and mount high and swing in a mighty circle and fall into their place again, a unit of a vast phalanx getting ready to be on the move. Day after day the observer in the swamps would have beheld these movements and marveled at them unless he was experienced enough with the ways of wild life to sense the import of it all.

How, and in what manner was the great hour of departure settled upon? How, indeed! It would be interesting to know. Sometimes the leader of this vast wilderness concourse would sound the warning note in the dead of night, sometimes in broad daylight, and instantly the army responded, not en masse, but by battalions that took the air, one after another, in quick succession. As they drifted off to the south they looked like ragged clouds that gradually assumed the V-shaped formation as they vanished on the horizon. To the hunter, left behind in the swamps, this V- shaped formation spelled "Good-Night!" "Adieu!" "Farewell—until next spring." And for years, in the spring, there reappeared in mighty V-shaped formation, over the fly- ways to the south and west these hosts of the air seeking old Beaver Lake, there to meet up with other thousands that had tested out their wings on a flight from breeding grounds in the Arctic circle! And what a clanking of voices as they greeted one another. It was enough to drive one raving distracted! The days of the twentieth century hold nothing comparable to the plenteous days of old Beaver Lake in her prime!

In a land once so abundantly stocked with all manner of wild game and visited annually by hunters from far and near, it is not surprising that the memory of the "old timer" still holds to traditions and tales of unusual occurrences in the way of freak shots. There is the tale of the frontiersman who dropped two deer running in opposite directions, with a solitary bullet.

They passed, or rather, met, at the opportune second and the bullet ploughed through them. There is the story of the man who shot a solitary goose and brought it down, only to have it fall into the open well of a solitary dweller of the marsh, thereby necessitating careful search on the part of the hunter. There are stories of unusual bags of game at a single shot on the part of the experienced hunter and the novice as well, for the game was so plentiful that almost anything could happen. Judge W. A. Hunter says that in all his many years' experience hunting on the river and in the marsh, the finest single shot he ever witnessed was made by that old-time artist, Pierre Brassard, of Momence. Pierre Brassard was a French-Canadian and one of the early settlers in the swamp environs of Momence. He knew every inch of the river and the Beaver Lake country, and, during his long experience, many a party of hunters from New York, Boston, Philadelphia and Chicago, representing the aristocracy of the fraternity of hunters, were piloted by him into this lake paradise.

Pierre and "Billy" were out on the river above Momence one day, located in "blinds," several hundred yards apart, when four lone geese appeared on the horizon. They came in "quartering," that is, on an angle with each bird fully exposed but, apparently, Pierre did not see them. Mr. Hunter says that, from his position, he could discern the gray top of Pierre's "musk-rat" cap inert and motionless above the weeds of the blind. Then, all in a second, the gray spot moved ever so slightly, the barrel of his gun slid up over the edge of the blind as if by magic, there was a report and one after another the four geese took a header towards the ground. He had killed all four at one shot. The impressive feature of this shot, said Mr. Hunter, was that it was calculated. He meant to drop all four birds at one shot and he did, Old Pierre was just that good with the gun.

Victor Brassard's face lighted with a knowing smile when he was reminded of the incident concerning the prowess of his father as a fine shot. "That," said he, "is peculiarly typical of father's style of shooting. I remember one day when father and a friend of his, and myself, went out on the river after ducks. We were located in "blinds," not far apart and father said: 'Now, I will take the first shot as they come over, and then you boys go after them.' But there was nothing to go after. The first ducks to appear were three in number, and father made a "pot shot" of them. Next) came two, and they fell likewise. AH of which goes to show that there is an instant when game in flight comes into alignment where the charge will prove most effective, and he knew just that second when to pull."

Over on the Kankakee, not so far away, in between "Bumbaloo" and French Island, there the old-timers still talk of Andy Granger's bag of thirty-three geese in the short space of forty minutes.

IV.

To fully appreciate this life of the old days in the open, one should have at some time in his career experienced not only the thrills of the hunter, but something of the weariness of a strenuous day's shooting from a boat or a "blind" in the marsh when the wind sang fine among the rushes and saw-grass and bore down the rain in fitful gusts— rain mixed with sleet—that stung the face and congealed the marrow in the bones. Hunting, even in the old days, was not "all beer and skittles." Even the faithful dog who ranged far and wide after every shot and brought in the birds that bulked high in the boat, was glad when he was "whistled in" and the boat's prow turned in the direction of home—home, in this case, being the snug little tent set under the protecting arms of a jack-oak on "Hog Island," or "Tater Island," or Pigeon Island," or some other island too poor to have a name. This tent in the marsh, after a long, hard day, gave a new meaning to the well-known lines of the poet:

"Be it ever so humble,

There's no place like home."

Generally, a fellow's hunting partner happened in about the same time. The day's kill was disposed of first, for there were men who did nothing else but haul the game thus killed to the railroad at Momence for shipment to Chicago. During the years of the early seventies, Frank Longpre did much of this hauling of game, and between loads would go out and knock down a goose or two himself. Citizen Silas Sink, a well-known resident of the lake region, earned the sobriquet of "Captain" by operating a small steamboat on the Kankakee river between Black Oak, in Indiana, and Momence, Illinois. It was a great convenience to the army of hunters in the swamp, for their game was regularly taken out and needed supplies brought in. During the seventies, one dozen fine mallards brought $1.00 to $1.75 in the Chicago market.

After the game had been attended to, then the sheet-iron stove was lighted and supper gotten under way. These suppers in the swamp camp were more or less elaborate affairs according to the culinary skill of those most concerned. A man out hunting all day and so busy that he could only snatch a "cold bite" now and then, landed in at night literally famished. A favorite expression used to be "that he could eat the inside out of a skunk." There was a generous pot of coffee, a spiderful of bacon and, if one's culinary accomplishments warranted so much, a batch of hot saleratus biscuits, together with such other accompaniments as the swamp larder contained.

After all, after a big day afield, battered and touseled by the winds and pelted by a cold rain, what is there that can approach the joy and creature comfort to be found in a snug, warm tent, a good supper of your own making, a pipeful of tobacco and a good pal to listen sympathetically as you relate the important incidents of the day? For most men of the old days that was just as near Heaven as a mortal could get this side of the pearly gates. And if one went so far as to take a swallow from a little brown bottle in those pre-Volstead days, it was just to propitiate the inner man. And if, perchance, before turning in for the night, he took still another "nip," that was merely a libation to the titular Gods of the wild to be generous with their gifts on the morrow. Decidedly there was a lure in the swamp life of the old days that touched a responsive chord in the generality of mankind. Lawyers, doctors, merchants, listened to the call of this great, outdoor play ground of Beaver Lake and responded in numbers.

There were times when justice languished in Kankakee for weeks at a time and patiently awaited the return of her chief representatives of the bar, T. P. Bonfield, C. A. Lake, Harrison Loring, Stephen R. Moore, William Potter, J. W. Paddock, and Judge Bartlett. Then there was "Uncle Pleas" Durham and Hugh Lancaster who chaperoned regularly a party of hunters who had grown old in the service but who, nevertheless, got a "kick" out of camp life and experienced a renewal of youth by the mere recital of old- time memories and a whiff of the game-laden southwest winds. The ammunition of this party was contained chiefly in suspicious brown jugs. None of them could sight a gun successfully, such were the infirmities of age, but they could appraise the spots of a deck of cards by candle light, and he who can do this is not hopelessly old. The limit was twenty- five cents. The shade who remembers when everybody else forgets, intimates that they never sought "the hay" until the "Wee, sma' hours." Now and then after they had turned in, the silence would be broken by a dry, racking, raucous cough, such a cough as would make Sir Harry Lauder feel as though his education in the matter of simulating a cough had been neglected. This was later followed by the explosive "wham" of the cork as it was pulled from the neck of the ammunition jug, the liquid ripple of spirits, the deep drawn sigh of satisfaction, and then—silence. Ah, memories, memories! A volume could be written of memories and nothing more of the great lake country in the days of its prime.

Men in those early days, particularly those who buffeted the swamps, were observant of everything about them. They were weather-wise to a degree that seemed uncanny all because they read the signs and took due notice thereof when nature gave intimation of a change of program. The old time hunter who has campaigned in the swamps wouldn't have particularly heeded the prophesies of the high-priced government official in Chicago today. Not he. He was used to casting his eye skyward in a broad, comprehensive sweep; he knew whether the sun at its rising or going down glowed red like a carbuncle, or was obscured by fogs and vapors; swiftly he noted the direction of the wind, whether the smoke rose straight up or hugged the ground; these indications are as infallible as a barometer. Then, too, the cirrocumuli of the meteorologist and the fleecy clouds of "the mackerel sky" of the swamp man were equally portentous.

In the marsh there were times when a significant hush fell upon the land, followed by a sudden puff of wind out of the southwest that bent the heads of the wild-rice sharply over and ruffled the water of the open spaces and then died away as suddenly as it came. If it were in the month of March, even though the sun were shining, the hunter wise to these out of door conditions knew there was something on the way, and acted accordingly. In an incredibly short time there would be wisps of thin, fleecy clouds mounting higher and higher, a freshening of the wind which in an hour's time, became a gale bearing an avalanche of snow or rain or sleet. Our friends of the wild always found a warning in the croak of the crow and the scream of the blue-jay.

Even the ponderous, reverberating notes of the swamp bull-frog were pregnant with meaning for the initiated. They seemed to say, "Better go 'round! Better go 'round! Better go 'round."

The "Black Marsh," to the north-east of the lake proper was a favorite breeding ground. Here, rising above the shallow waters of the marsh by the hundreds, so thick that they suggested hay-cocks in a meadow, were the unique habitations of the musk-rats. Other contiguous swamps were similarly inhabited. Here, also, the geese in the spring, with an eye to utility and convenience, made use of the materials already provided by the industrious rats, and made their nests on the roof of his dwelling without so much as intimating "By your leave." A strange and interesting combination it was—rats within and geese without—sometimes as many as five or six of them in close proximity to one another, on the same curious mound of dried weeds and rushes. These unbidden guests of the wild when disturbed by the hunter or the near approach of his dog, would curve their long necks downward and with heads close to the water, slide easily and gracefully in, after which they voiced a noisy protest at being disturbed.

The mallards, more particular as to situation and more skillful in the matter of building their nests, built among the rushes and cat-tails and the rice, of which they made use in anchoring their nests in a peculiar way. A mallard's nest was made large at the bottom, tapering to a considerable height where the nest was located. The foundation materials were woven loosely about several upstanding rushes or cat-tails, so that the nest could rise or lower with the flood waters of the slough.

Ordinarily one would think that it could not possibly matter whether a nest rose or fell with the tide or not. But the logic of the wild, that unerring instinct which guides certain of the water-fowl, disproves all this. Supposing the nest were firmly anchored and the waters of the slough receded so that the nest was suspended six inches above the surface of the water. The young ducklings might fall out into the water all right, but how would they ever get back home and under mother's protecting wing? With the nest thus anchored, but able to rise and lower with the waters, it rode the waves safely when the surface was lashed by heavy winds. Otherwise the nest would have been inundated. The sloping sides served an important end in this scheme of the wilderness household. By this means the young ducks were enabled to reach the water easily, and just as easily come from the water back into the nest.

During July and August the wild life of the marsh was most interesting to observe. Multitudes of musk-rats, as if conscious that their fur coats were of little value to the hunter at that time of the year, disported in numbers about the sedgy margins of the swamp. Myriads of young mallards, half grown, foraged here and there and even contested with the rats for certain choice tid-bits of marsh floatsam picked up in their wanderings. The stringy, bulbous root of the swamp artichoke was a morsel much sought by rats and ducks alike, and many a tug-of-war occurred between these opposing forces—a rat at one end and a duck at the other. The musk-rats were so numerous that they would run five hundred to the acre in the opinion of the old- time hunter. As to the mallards—there was absolutely no way in which a man could arrive at a reasonable estimate of their numbers. The homing phase of wild life was interesting to observe, and the old-timer recalls how these young, half-grown mallards, at nightfall, sought out the old nest and as many as could perched on its precipitous sides, while the balance, if the family were large—say about a dozen—sat in the water with their feet drawn up into the soft feathers of the breast, and with heads tucked under their wings dreamed of polly-wogs and bugs.

The Beaver Lake region not only attracted huge flights of ducks, geese and swan, but here, also, was the home primeval of the picturesque sand-hill crane. They frequented this section literally by the thousands. Every hunter of pioneer days has some story to rev late-concerning a peculiar ceremonial observed by these birds in the spring and sometimes in the early fall, which is often alluded to as the "dance of the cranes." At such times numbers of these birds gathered on a high spot of the prairie adjacent to the water. They formed in a circle, each one equi-distant from his neighbor, and thus disposed they went through a series of movements strangely akin to the figures of a quadrille. Always there was a dignity of movement and a seriousness of mien and deportment altogether amusing, interesting and quite out of the ordinary. One of the movements most generally recalled by those who have witnessed them, is that which resembled "leap-frog." The bird ahead would squat close to the ground while the one behind would vault lightly over. Immediately on alighting, this bird would crouch down to the ground while the other jumped over.

Beaver Lake was a body of water seven miles long and about five miles wide and from six to nine feet deep, situated mainly in McClellan township, Newton county, Indiana. Contiguous swamps added vastly to this area which was known generally as "The Beaver Lake Country." In 1853 the state of Indiana undertook to reclaim a portion of this swamp tract by running a ditch from the northwest corner of the lake to the Kankakee river, several miles away to the north. This effort was pretty much of a failure as it only caused the shore-line of the lake to recede by about one hundred yards. Twenty-five to thirty years later Lemuel Milk, of Kankakee, the well-known land magnate, became interested in the project of draining this vast tract, and went after it with characteristic energy. The old ditch was widened and deepened and its carrying capacity increased. The limestone "hog-back" above Momence, Illinois, was cut through and the Kankakee, with its flood thus released, made short work of draining picturesque Beaver Lake.

While the success of this great reclamation project was being acclaimed by the public in general, tragedy was stalking abroad in all the vast realm where, from time immemorial, had dwelt the feathered legions of the wild. In the nesting places of the shallow swamps the geese had but recently brought off their broods, all unmindful of impending disaster. There were tens of thousands of these big, soft, fuzzy goslings suddenly bereft of their native element—water. Goslings at best are poor "land-lubbers" but fine sailors and aeronauts once they are supplied with water and wing-feathers, but in this case they had neither. The sight was pitiable, says A. L. Barker, who, as a boy witnessed it all. They walked and rolled and dragged themselves painfully to the few depressions in the marsh bottom where water still remained and crowded these places to suffocation. For days the sandy spaces roundabout the sloughs were alive with the roly-poly forms of these goslings, some dead, others dying, while the remainder toiled persistently though painfully landward, under a burning sun, in search of water. The helplessness and misery of these hapless waifs of the wild would have moved a soul of adamant to pity. The mother geese were everywhere encouraging their flocks as best they might, but the task was a hopeless one and one after another they fell by the wayside. Only the stronger ones and such as were helped endured and reached the life-saving water in the door-yard of the swamp settler. It was a disaster so far-reaching in its effects upon the wild life of the region that man was helpless to succor them except in a very limited way. Mr. Barker recalls that he picked up numbers of these goslings and bore them to a place of safety in his father's barnyard, and that the mother geese, so far from being perturbed by the presence of man, apparently sensed that it was an act of mercy. As the goslings wallowed in the puddles about the watering trough the old geese would stretch their necks and wag their heads up and down unruffled by the approach of a stranger, meanwhile giving voice to a delightfully soft and friendly little "croak" which, in the language of wild meant, beyond a doubt—"Thank you, mister, thank you for your kindness."

The geese were not the only ones to suffer. With the passing of the waters of the lake the hosts of buffalo, cat-fish and pickerel contained therein were left marooned in shallow pools or stranded helplessly in the black muck of the lake's bottom. There were buffalo and pickerel of enormous size, patriarchs of these primeval waters, whose carcasses littered the bottom of the lake so thickly that one could step from one to another in any direction, like upon so many stepping stones. For weeks, after the release of the waters, this spot was like a charnel house, from which emanated odors of fish and game, rotting under the rays of a hot sun, that smelled to Heaven and hung over this citadel of the wilderness like a pestilential blanket. Man had won in the conflict with nature! The citadel had fallen!

V.

Austin Dexter is a marsh inhabitant who has spent eighty-six years there. He was born at Rensselaer, Indiana, in 1839, and shortly after his people moved into the lake country and he has been there ever since. He

AN ANCIENT "SWAMP-RAT" Austin Dexter, at the Right in the Picture, is, Perhaps, Beaver Lake's Oldest Citizen in Point of Continuous Residence. He Came to the Lake as a Baby and is Now Eighty-Six Years Old. He has Visions of the Lake Country Again Returning to a State of Nature in Time. is what is known in the expressive phraseology of the lake country as "a Swamp-Rat." Life, in the main, has been uneventful save that it is rich in the garnered experiences of the little realm in which he has so long lived and moved and been a part. In his little hut back among the oaks of a sand-ridge, not far from the famous "Shafer Ridge," we found him and talked with him. Here he lives during the summer, pretty much by himself, and, in the winter he goes down to Kentland a pensioner on the bounty of Newton county. His recollection of the marsh goes back into the early forties. The Pottawattomi were there in that day and, with their primitive weapons, were the principal hunters for a time. His oldei* brother spent much time with them and became quite expert in speaking and under-standing the Pottawattomi tongue. In that day, besides the aquatic life that filled the marsh, there were countless deer and wolves that ranged the adjacent prairie and oak- scrub of the sand-ridges. He recalls that during the fifties and the sixties hunters made a business of hunting deer for the market. He has beheld wagon loads of deer carcasses piled high and tied with ropes, ready for transport to market at Rensselaer or Morocco, In diana, or across the line into Illinois to Momence.

There is a tradition associated with the year he was born, 1839, of which he likes to tell. The winter was very severe and many deer took refuge on Big Bogus Island. During the protracted season of cold the waters of the lake were frozen over and then the citizens of the region inaugurated a big drive. Nearly everybody in the neighborhood participated in the affair, men, boys and a woman or two, more hardy and venturesome than the rest, joined in the sport. This wilderness posse was armed with rifles, pitch-forks, corn-knives—anything that might serve as a weapon. The grass of the island was fired and the deer, driven before the wall of fire, emerged in numbers upon the glare ice of the lake. Then the slaughter ensued for the deer, unable to stand on the slippery surface of the lake, sprawled in every direction in their mad efforts to escape and became easy victims. It is said that the bag of game in that drive amounted to seventy head of deer, a fox or two and six or seven wolves. It was a big event in the lake's history.

AN ANCIENT SWAMP RAT

Austin Dexter, at the right in the picture is, perhaps, Beaver Lake's oldest citizen in point of continuous residence. He came to the lake as a baby and is now eighty-six years old he has visions of the lake country again returning to a state of nature in time.

Naturally, there are memories etched on the very soul of this ancient swamp recluse of days when the wildlife of the upper air concentrated here. Again, a man would have profited if he had known something of the prodigal abundance of these wilderness days, for Austin Dexter, though friendly and willing, was disposed to listen rather than talk, and this reticence was due in a large measure to the fact that tales of the Lake's early days now seem extravagant, overdrawn, improbable. By degrees, however, he talked—talked in the halting monosyllable of the marsh- man—of nights in the early spring when the feathered hosts of the air came tumbling in. Many and many is the night he says, that he has lain awake in his shack, unable to sleep from the incessant "cac, cac, cac," of the redheads and mallards mingled with the wild, strident "honk" of geese, belated travelers of the night who sought a resting spot in this wilderness hostelry.

As these hosts settled down, they disturbed still other hosts so that the night was a perfect bedlam of distracting cries, so much so that sleep was entirely out of the question. There were times when the swamp's feathered denizens, from some unknown source and in some unaccountable way, were warned of some untoward thing and rose en masse. It was a sight awe-inspiring, spectacular, sublime, and the noise of untold thousands of wings beating the air in unison as they arose from the water reverberated in the timber- fringed confines of the lake like heavy thunder. Such old-time hunters of the swamps as Victor Brassard, Wm. A. Hunter and Tom Magruder, say that these sudden, unexplain-able upheavals of game taking wing at the same instant, registered on the sensibilities like the reverberations of a mild explosion

A fellow's nerves would farly tingle for a time as from the effects of a mighty electric shock.

As he spoke of these happenings of the past his eye ranged slowly the vast expanse of country to the south where, traced in the swamp bottoms, were staring highways of white, farms fenced in and fields of corn white from the early autumn frosts, where formerly the boats of the hunters plied. To the southeast of "Big Bogus" laid the deep sink of old Beaver Lake. His eye rested here while he pointed out the huge dredge-ditch, its precipitous sides covered for the most part with scrub-oak, sumach and briers, through which shone dully, patches of dead, gray quicksand. It was then the tragedy of the swamp stood revealed. Through this ditch the heart's blood of old Beaver Lake had drained to the last drop. "They murdered this land while they were at it," said Austin Dexter sadly, "and made a good job of it!" Its primitive voices are stilled, unless we except the lugubrious voice of the crow and the chattering of the black-bird hosts. Man has deliberately sacrificed the plenty that here fell regularly from the hand of the Almighty and, in return, drew a burden of taxes.

FAMOUS "BOGUS ISLAND"

Beaver Lake and Bogus Island are but memories in this day. It is difficult for the casual visitor to realize that this was a swamp region, thousands of acres in extent, whose deep retreats were frequented by counterfeiters, horse thieves, murderers and criminals of lesser degree. So changed is the land that only the campaigner of its old days may know with something of certainty "just where he is at," in this lifeless, wide open land of today.

The term lifeless is meant only in a relative sense, as indicating the entire absence of the hosts of wild fowl that once made this wilderness retreat vocal with their cries as they passed in and out. The chatter of the blackbird hosts is but the feeble echo of wilderness life of the long ago. The south-west winds are empty today save where they pick up the dry sands of the old lake bed and weave them in spirals and sift them in soft, gray diaphanous clouds until, ir the distance, they seem like spirit-flights of the ancient hosts of the wild haunting this spot of many memories.

Within forty years section lines have been run, fences built and a perfect checkerboard of stone roads built in the very heart of this swamp region. Its famous secret places are secret no longer, but have been opened to the public in the most ruthless and unfeeling manner and then forgotten, apparently, save by the "swamp-rat," to whom the whole thing is a nightmare—nay, more—a tragedy. "Little Bogus" and "Big Bogus" Islands, famous as the rendezvous of the early-day banditti, loom upon the landscape amid quiet pastoral scenes that afford little or no background for the fierce tales of the border credited to them. The island's most formidable protecting barrier today is the unromantic but practical "barbed-wire" fence.

This island, which is several acres in extent and wooded, was occupied as early as 1836 by counterfeiters, who made quantities of spurious coin which they circulated on the outside by means of confederates and helpers. The Illinois country was alive with horse thieves and counterfeiters. They were even more numerous than the "hold-up" men of today. There is a tradition that three counterfeiters were arrested on Little Bogus in 1837. They were taken before Justice Wesley Spitler, tried and bound over to the circuit court. They forfeited their bonds and the case never came to trial.

A horse stolen from the neighborhood of Milford, Illinois in 1857 was followed by a posse of twelve or fifteen men to the neighborhood of Bogus Island. The thief, hard pressed, left the horse in the timber and made an unsuccessful attempt to escape. He was discovered crossing the big ditch a little way north of the bridge that crosses the ditch near the Jennie M. Conrad home, and, as he emerged on the other side, the bullets of the pursuing party dropped him in his tracks. Apparently the formality of an inquest was dispensed with. He was a known horse thief, and that was enough. They did drag the body to the top of the sightly sand-hill and buried it there. This eminence is known today as "Horse Thief Hill." About this time, too, "Old Shafer," a swamp character with a most sinister record, variously known as "Mike" or "William," was arrested. He was afterwards tried for harboring thieves and stolen property, and was sentenced to three years in the penitentiary.

LITTLE BOGUS ISLAND"

There is Nothing About This Modest Little Oak-Crowned Island of Today That Even Hints of Tenants as Fearsome as the Horse Thief and the Counterfeiter. Eighty Years ago, it was a Stronghold Surrounded by Water and Frequented by Desperate Men. Many a Stolen Horse has Been Secreted Here.

Early day citizens of Momence were obliged to wage constant and unrelenting warfare on these undesirables, and to that end the services of Col. Phil Worcester, "Uncle Sid" Vail and Walter B. Hess were enlisted on behalf of the community during a period of years and with something of success. In 1839, at a point on "Big Bogus" Island, on its southeastern side where the sandy promontory rises from the bed of the old lake, a point still distinguished by a huge oak tree, there Col. Worcester and his party surprised a band of five counterfeiters and made them captives. Tradition, which is vague and shadowy, says that the Worcester party consisted of himself, Sid Vail and "Uncle Billy" Nichols, with James Graham for a guide. They came across in a boat from Hunter's Point, to the south-west of the island, in the darkness of the night, guided only by a beacon light which shone from high up in the oak tree. The very audacity of the scheme made it successful. The counterfeiters were sure they were welcoming some of their own party instead of officers of the law.

Walter B. Hess, almost from the first day he became a resident of the border settlement of Momence, identified himself prominently with this movement to preserve law and order. He had a most formidable antagonist in the wiley Shafer whom he at last landed back of the bars for a three-year term. But Shafer had a long memory, he was cunning and revengeful, and in the end Mr. Hess lost many and many a good horse and, apparently, was helpless to avert it. Then, there were the brothers, Shep and Wright Latin who had the run of the town and were concerned in many a shady transaction. Mr. Hess never charged Shep Latin with actual stealing, but his clever brain hatched many a scheme which worked out to the great detriment of people of the community with good, likely horses. Shep Latin was really a likable fellow; not vindictive like "Old Shafer." Mr. Hess says that Wright Latin one day went by his house with five horses, which afterwards proved to have been stolen. A day or so later several men came by hunting for them and Mr. Hess gave the fellows such directions as he was able. A day or so later the men returned bringing four horses with them. They said they could not find the fifth horse but found a man in charge of the four. They added significantly that his horse stealing days were over. The description they gave of the man tallied exactly with that of Wright Latin, and he was never heard from later. Many years later, while some men were digging a ditch near Blue Grass, in Indiana, they were very much frightened on exhuming a skeleton. It was, in all probability, the remains of Wright Latin.

The story is told how one day, while Shep Latin was intoxicated, he said to Mr. Hess:

"Hess you're a fool to work as you do. I can put you in the way of making an easier living—just look at this." Whereupon he pulled out of several pockets handfuls of bills, with the remark: "My clothes are just lined with money."

Mr. Hess refused his confidences on this and other occasions. Summing up his life work in the matter of searching out criminals, however, he was quite positive that, if he were a young man again going into a border country he would not take the active part he did in trying to break up lawlessness. Once he pursued a horse thief for three weeks and in the chase ruined a better horse than the one that had been stolen.

"BIG BOGUS ISLAND"

Since the Draining of the Waters of Beaver Lake, "Big Bogus" Looms on its Southeastern Side like a Huge Promontory of Sand. The Figure to the Right in the Picture is Standing on the Spot Where a Gang of Early-Day Counterfeiters Had Their "Dugout." At This Point Five of a Gang Were Captured by Col. Worcester and a Band of Momence Men

105

"Little Bogus," which was the favorite haunt of counterfeiters and thieves, was reached from the west and northwest by lonely trails, obscure and winding. It was surrounded on all sides by deep water which made surprise attack by officers of the law out of the question. By many of the marsh residents it was suspected that there was an easier way into it than by swimming one's horse through the deep waters surrounding it, and, at the time the waters of Beaver Lake were drained, there was brought to light for the first time a peculiar configuration of the lake bottom.

From the island's highest point today the observer beholds, stretching away to the north-west, the ziz-zag lines of a narrow "hog-back" of sand which, lying close to the surface of the lake yet obscured by the water, afforded easy means of ingress and egress to men on horseback familiar with the peculiar lay of the land. From the point where the "hog-back" stopped abruptly, there was an interval of deep water between it and the adjacent sand-ridge to the west of some three or four hundred feet.

Evidences of an early day engineering feat were unearthed at this point years ago at the time when one of the lateral ditches was dredged through. The dredge discovered with its steel nose a roadway constructed of logs six to eight inches in diameter, placed side by side corduroy fashion.

This submerged corduroy roadway was laid in a shallow spot in the lagoon, and reached from the sand-ridge on the west as far as the "hog-back," several hundred feet away to the south-east. Long after the waters of the lake had been drained away, this connecting bit of road, deeply embedded in the swamp muck, was clearly visible.

THE SPOT OF THE CORDUROY ROAD

This bit of Beaver Lake Scenery Lies in Between "Little Bogus" and the High Land to the Left. Here is Where the Corduroy Road was Found Which Connected the Ridge with a Submerged "Hog-Back" That Extended to the Northwest from the Island.

One may behold it all today clearly revealed in the sunshine, the winding highway of the early-day banditti and the dip to the sand-ridge where the corduroy road was laid. It is an innocent looking bit of sandy surface today even though it once formed an important link for those who sought the island stronghold.

"Bogus Island" in its primitive days, was as snug and secure a place as was ever hit upon by the fugitive from justice, or he whose questionable practices thrive best in secret. Covered by a thick growth of oak and brush, its shores fringed about by a dense growth of cat-tails and wild rice, surrounded by deep water, uncharted save for the secret submerged trail to the north-west, what more secure haven could have been desired? Midway of the island, at the head of a small ravine which dips sharply to the east, is today a hole in the ground which popular tradition fixes as the spot where the counterfeiters had their cabin of logs and carried on their operations. The sandy area about this spot has yielded, in the course of the years, many mementoes in the way of spurious coins and counterfeiter's paraphernalia. Here, and at "Big Bogus," three miles to the south-east, as the crow flies, was the rallying point for these underworld characters of border days who, for years continued to be a thorn in the side of the border settlement at Momence. They were clever men, desperate men, who, in the pinch, held human life cheaply, so that in the category of crimes directly chargeable to them, there sometimes occurred the charge of murder. There are tales still told which lack much of detail and color, and legends vague and various touching upon the lives and doings of the banditti of the swamps, bandied about among the older folk of the region. But, for the most part time has wiped the memory clean of all definite recollection of these stirring events, with the possible exception of the chief bandit himself—"Old Shafer," who forms the subject of a special story to follow.

Dr. John F. Shronts, the well-known pioneer doctor of Momence, as a young man just out of college, sought a location for the practice of his profession near to the cross-roads where stands the hamlet of Lake Village, Indiana. Here, in the heart of the Beaver Lake country, he occupied a primitive log cabin and hung out his shingle as M. D. as early as 1868 or 1869. Here, for years, he practiced, later removing to Momence, Illinois. A queer place, you may think, for a young doctor to light upon, a place without prospect or future, whose inhabitants, in the main, were of the criminal stripe and desperate. But the facts are these men were just as susceptible to chills and fever and "swamp ague" as the "squatter" trapper and woodsman, of whom, to use the vernacular of the marsh of that day, "thar wuz a considerable sprinkling." There was a broken arm and broken leg, now and then, to be adjusted and at such times when the boys of questionable character and calling celebrated a successful "haul" on the outside by raising highjinks in their island stronghold for days at a time—when liquor flowed freely and enthusiasm ran high—not infrequently the lone doctor was sought by them to treat a gun-shot wound or repair a damage caused by fists. Boys will be boys, and the best of friends fall out now and then!

Dr. Shronts used to recall that, on his first visit to the secret places of the island banditti, he was obliged to submit to being blind-folded on going in and coming out of the place. In the course of the years, however, this precaution was dispensed with. For years he knew of the secret "hog-back highway" but was unable to locate it by his own knowledge unaided. But the Doctor concerned himself only in his profession and was careful not to show too great an interest in the past life and doings of his patients. Withal, he was discreet, cautious, careful not to let drop the least hint of gossip or criticism relating to the affairs of this underworld clientele so that in the end he held their confidence as no other man of the lake region ever did. Long after he had removed to Momence, Dr. Shronts was called by the swamp folk generally, in time of need, and by members of the island banditti particularly whenever the emergency arose. By day and by night he traveled the precarious footing of "Lyon's Lane," to still more precarious and uncertain trails which wound about through thicket and scrub and miniature sand-dunes, and which led, finally to the humble cabin of the trapper and hunter or the more isolated abodes of the "Bogus Island" bandits. It was a faithful service he rendered these habitants of the Lake region during all the days he lived— summer or winter in fair weather and foul, day or night.

The incident is recalled of one occasion when Dr. Shronts was out of town, a messenger from Bogus Island sought him on behalf of one of their number who had been kicked by a horse. In the absence of Dr. Shronts his colleague, Dr. H. M. Keyser, was appealed to. The Doctor was reluctant at first to undertake the trip for the reputation of the prospective patient, a habitue of "Little Bogus," was not altogether reassuring. In his professional experience he had had but little to do with them. The messenger offered him a double fee, but the Doctor soon made it clear that his unwillingness, in this case, was not so much a matter of the fee as it was a matter of safety for himself and his horse. "Supposing," said the Doctor, "that someone of your number fancied my horse and helped himself to it? What a predicament I would be in! What assurance have I that this will not happen?" The messenger smiled grimly and replied, "When men of our stripe give a promise they live up to it. Should your horse be stolen, I promise that you will be supplied with a better one! I will take you in and bring you back, and pay you well besides." And, thus assured, Dr. Keyser made the trip to Bogus Island. And these men of shady reputation and desperate character treated him royally.

The passing of Dr. John F. Shronts in many respects was marked like the closing of an epoch—like the last chapter in a tale of stirring events of red-blood days brought to a point where the frontier "faded out" and present day civilization began. What wealth of stirring reminiscence and thrilling incident of the old, lawless days of the lake country passed beyond mortal ken with the passing of the old Doctor, we can only surmise. We do know that it was considerable and that its loss to the generation of today is irreparable.

"OLD SHAFER" OF THE KANKAKEE MARSH

Verily, the way of the transgressor is hard; and to him that showeth not mercy, in the end mercy shall be denied. To make use of still another truism evolved from the sum of human experiences throughout the ages, "He who lives by the sword shall perish by the sword." "Old Shafer," of the black Marsh, as the country contiguous to famous "Bogus Island" over the line in Indiana, was known in the early days, was a most sinister and forbidding character. He was an outlaw steeped in crime, who ruled the isolated swamp region of the Kankakee Marshes with an iron hand. Where the law of organized society had not permeated in that early day he was a law unto himself, and many a thief, counterfeiter and assassin found asylum there when pressed too hard by the civil authorities. "Old Shafer," as he was known far and wide, was not old in years. He was old in crime hence the title, "Old Shafer." Apparently there was no crime in the criminal calendar of that day, from petty larceny to murder, of which "Old Shaf." was not guilty.

Moreover, he sometimes boasted of it, shocking as the statement may seem.

Where Mike Shafer came from no one knows. That part of his life is a sealed book. He operated from famous "Shafer Ridge," in the Beaver Lake country during the fifties and up until his death in 1869. By many it is said that he began his operations there as far back as 1844. The gossip of that early day in the swamps credited him with being a man of unusual attainments in the matter of education. He is said to have been a graduate of one of the great eastern colleges.

That Mike Shafer was not his real name but an assumed one, there can be little doubt. Opinion of the countryside, however, is a unit in ascribing to him the doubtful honor of being one of the most formidable outlaws that ever operated in the Mississippi valley in a day when the frontier gave asylum to the worst of them. He made his word the law in the little domain in which he operated and he enforced that law in the most vigorous and summary manner. That he was for so long a thorn in the side of the little frontier settlement of Momence, that he so long eluded successfully the clutches of the law, is a tribute at once to his nerve, cunning and consummate skill by which he directed the underworld forces under his command.

Mrs. Nutt and Mrs. Alzada Hopper, now residents of Momence, were the daughters of Hugh Williamson. Williamson was a hunter who, in 1863, left Kankakee City and took up his abode in the Kankakee marshes with his family. In that early day the "Beaver Lake" region, as it was known, was a hunter's paradise with its thousands of acres of swampy stretches studded with musk-rat houses, and flanked by wild-rice and towering cat-tails and bulrushes. Here and there an island appeared and these were heavily timbered with oak and tangled, almost impenetrable scrub- oak. As a breeding ground and natural retreat for wild game this ancient habitat has seldom been equaled and never surpassed anywhere in the Mississippi basin.

In the days of the early sixties when Williamson took up his abode there, the wild deer were still very plentiful and numbers of them fell before his rifle. There were times when he would load the wide pole-rack of his wagon with the carcasses of deer, piling them high, one upon the other like cord-wood, and take them to Momence, where he disposed of them to the butcher shops, stores, or anyone wanting them. At other times when the local markets had been well supplied, he sought Chicago, fifty miles away. It was a day when venison held its own with the products of a gradually developing civilization, and more often than not the carcass of a deer held the place of vantage on a hook outside the market door.

Years before Williamson took up his abode in the marsh and built his primitive log cabin on the ridge to the north-east of "Little Bogus," the counterfeiters and horse thieves had established their headquarters within its protecting environs. Here from as far back as the early thirties, they carried on successfully their nefarious business and, apparently, gave little heed to the humble hunter or trapper so long as he showed the good sense to keep a bridle on his tongue, and did not interest himself too much in their affairs or try to see too much. Among these dwellers of the marsh region who made a vocation of hunting and trapping, the sinister qualities of their associates were recognized in a way, and popular gossip attributed to each certain dark and devious pursuits as well as certain crimes of which they whispered furtively and cautiously among themselves. The "grape-vine telegraph" of that day was an effective disseminator of the "news" of this underworld retreat, and these tales as they passed from one to another, lost not one jot nor tittle, but gained in interesting detail as they made the rounds. These tales were not mere fabrications altogether; a thread of fact and truth ran through them all.

Mrs. Nutt and her sister, Mrs. Hopper, as girls in this frontier stronghold knew "Old Shafer." He was sometimes a caller at their cabin where he conversed with their father. Mrs. Nutt recalls that he was a powerful man, with a good head and as fine and regular a set of teeth as any man was ever blessed with. To her father he remarked one day: "Williamson, I shot a man once, and all I could shake out of him was a dollar!" "That might sound like bravado," said Mrs. Nutt, "but you cannot make me believe but "Old Shafer" told the truth for once." If other tales concerning him are to be given similar credence then, somewhere amid the low-lying sand dunes and scrub-oak isles that surrounded his cabin there is secreted to this day a nail-keg containing a goodly quantity of gold pieces— the sum of the profits yielded to this master criminal during a lifetime. So persistent was the story of this hidden wealth that, after his death, search was made for it in and about the place but without success. There were casks containing pork and beef, but the fabled nail-keg and its treasure is still undiscovered.

But the legend of the nail-keg and its contents of golden eagles still lives in the memory of the countryside, and, after the lapse of half a century, there are those who believe that someone, sometime, more lucky than the rest will stumble upon it by accident. You ask an old-time resident of the marsh country and he will tell you that most certainly "Old Shafer" left a quantity of gold secreted somewhere. No question about that. Years ago there were those of the older residents who avowed by all that was good and great that they had beheld the ghost of "Old Shafer" on certain nights prowling among the oaks in the near vicinity of his cabin home, one end of which was dug into the side of a sand-dune. Not one but several claim to have beheld these nocturnal visitations by the spectral figure of "Old Shafer," on some special mission bent, and once when the moonlight glinting through an open space in the oaks fell full upon the massive back, lo, there appeared the gaping gunshot wound, evidence enough for any reasonable person that the wraith was that of Shafer and no one else. Little wonder that these simple folk of the swamps should spin these phantasies of the formidable Shafer and clothe his memory with attributes approaching the supernatural.

Notable among the varied accomplishments attributed to "Old Shafer" was his ability to change distinguishing spots and marks on a horse. Many maintain that such was the excellence of his art that he could transform a white horse into a bright bay, or a bay to glossy chestnut or black. He was a wizard, deep and uncanny, whose operations in this line still linger in the memory of the swamp folk whose gossip and legends concerning him are as varied and colorful as the best examples of work ever turned out by this master hand. Shafer's cabin home was situated two miles west and one and one- quarter miles south of the village of Rose Lawn, Indiana, on an oak-studded sand-ridge that bears the name of "Shafer's Ridge" to this day. This ridge laid along the northern edge of what was termed "The Black Marsh," and was some five or six miles distant from the rendezvous of the horse thieves on "Big Bogus" island to the south. He thus maintained the appearance of having no connection with the band on "Big Bogus" island, but was conveniently near to lend a hand in their operations.

Frequently a stolen horse with marks so prominent as to make identification easy, was run through the marsh to Shafer's "studio," in the brush, there to undergo such changes as the exigencies of the case made necessary or advisable. Shafer's practiced eye and skillful hand soon transformed the tell-tale marks so that one might go with an animal thus treated out into the highways of the world with little fear of detection. Of course, the transformation was accomplished by means of dyes. These dyes were of his own concocting and were brewed from certain barks and roots found in the wild. Austin Dexter, whose eighty years of continuous residence in the marsh and whose knowledge of Shafer's methods entitle him to consideration, rather scouts the idea that Shafer went so far as to change the color of a horse entirely. In most cases it would not be necessary. When it came to changing the spots on an animal, however, he was very skillful. A likely looking horse that needed only a white star in the forehead to completely baffle description, was treated in a unique manner. The animal's head was first firmly secured between two posts and then a boiled potato, hot out of the kettle, would be bound to the forehead and left long enough to blister the skin, so that the hair would fall out. After five or six weeks the scar healed and the new hair that came in was always white, and the star thus produced was a permanent one.

That blackest of all crimes included in the criminal repertoire of "Old Shafer," was when he deliberately murdered his youngest daughter. This girl of ten years observed the unusual operations that went on about her, and was curious and questioning, after the manner of a child, but, despite numerous warnings to be silent, she prattled innocently of it all in the presence of strangers. One day when a posse in search of two stolen horses stopped at Shafer's place, they questioned him closely concerning them. The old bandit stoutly denied having seen them, although in reality they had passed through his hands several days before, when suddenly the girl exclaimed: "Why, papa, don't you remember those men with the horses who stopped her only day before yesterday?" He cuffed the girl soundly and told her to go about her business. He then did some tall lying in order to extricate himself, although the men in the posse were far from satisfied, and regarded the incident of the girl as significant. Shafer's rage knew no bounds and then and there he resolved to make away with the child. Shortly after that, on the pretext of picking blue-berries which grew abundantly on the sandy intervals of the marsh, Shafer and the girl left the cabin. Shafer returned alone but the girl was never seen again.

He cut her throat with a butcher knife, at least that is the legend of the swamps, and tearing out her hair he scattered it in handfuls in a lonely spot in the scrub to make it appear that she had been attacked and devoured by the wolves. Shafer's oldest daughter, (he had but two), believed the story of the father implicitly. Later, when the mother was on her death bed, she called the girl to her and, drawing her close whispered the awful details of the father's crime and urged her to fly from the accursed spot to a place of safety. Dismayed, overwhelmed by this startling intelligence, the daughter did as she was directed and ran away, but not until the mother, after repeated urging, commanded her to. "I can't die but once," said the mother to the weeping girl; "for me the end is not far off; but you—you who will still live when I am gone, what can there be for you in this hell-hole of iniquity but sorrow? So, fly, fly. Go as far away as you can and—forget, forget this horrid thing—forget everything, everything, except that your mother loved you." And thus, obeying a mother's injunction "Old Shafer's" daughter set her face resolutely to the south and made her way slowly, carefully, cautiously out of the great Kankakee swamps in quest of that mystic land where, perchance, happiness might be found. One John Coffelt, helped the girl as far as the Wabash, and from that far-off day until the present no word has ever been received from her. John Coffelt was a son of Justice Coffelt who, at that time, lived on the edge of the swamp. Justice Coffelt had at one time bound Shafer over to the grand jury on a charge of harboring stolen horses. In some manner it came to the knowledge of Shafer that John Coffelt had aided his daughter in her flight. The result of it all was that in a short time Coffelt lost nine head of horses. Such was the effectiveness of the book-keeping system employed by this thief of long memory and implacable mood.

After the departure of his daughter and the death of his wife, who did not long survive, Shafer was left alone save for such company of his own peculiar "stripe" who now and then sought him out on business bent. If he sometimes thought of the past, if sometimes he fled from his own thoughts, terror stricken after sleepless nights, when the shades of his many victims walked in ghastly procession before his staring eyes, the "grapevine telegraph" of the dunes and swamps gave not the slightest hint or intimation. Rather, there was increased activity on the part of all the sinister forces harbored within the protecting confines of the "Beaver Lake" country, and "Old Shafer's" keen mentality and indefatigable energy were behind many a successful raid.

Mr. Walter B. Hess, of Momence, whose citizenship dates back to 1839, was, for many years, head of the law and order forces that made war on the banditti of the "Bogus Island" stronghold. He it was who succeeded in conducting the Danville authorities into the place. A horse thief was shot and "Old Shafer" was arrested. Shafer served a short term in the penitentiary as a result of this raid but on his return, he took up his nefarious business where he had left off. Such was the strength of his vengeance, such the cunning and devilish ingenuity he exercised that in the twelve years following his release from the penitentiary Mr. Hess lost fifty-three head of horses poisoned, shot, cut to pieces and stolen. One night his barn east of Momence was entered and eight horses contained therein were poisoned. Two of these had their tails cut off and they were otherwise mutilated. The barn was still locked on the following morning. And "Old Shafer" gloated over the toll he had exacted from his arch enemy, for these raids had been conducted with such consummate skill that not the slightest trace had been left by which the legal authorities could reach him.

After a life of crime which extended over many years, during which he served a short jail sentence or two, "Old Shafer" fell by the same means he had so often employed. He was shot in the back at short range, the charge of buckshot tearing a frightful hole in his body and dropping him in his tracks. Details as given by the swamp folk are meager and conflicting. One report has it that Shafer's assassin crept up to his cabin in the early dusk of March and shot through the window while he was engaged in frying a panful of bacon over the open blaze of the fireplace; that he lunged head first into and face downwards into the blaze atop of the frying-

pan, and that when found some time later, the fire had
burned out but not before it had burned the upper part of
Shafer's body until it was a black, charred mass, almost
unrecognizable. Mrs. Nutt and Mrs. Hopper give quite
another version. Shafer was shot in the back at close range as
he was about to enter his cabin. At the entrance to his cabin
there were two or three log steps placed in a shallow area-way
that led down to the door, and "Old Shafer" stood on the
topmost of these steps when the fatal shot was fired. In his
right hand he held the bail of a small iron kettle and in his
left, clutched in a death-grip, was an old dish-rag. The
assassin gathered leaves and small branches with which he
surrounded the body as it laid there, and set them on fire with
the evident intention of cremating the body of the old bandit
in his own premises. The leaves burned out but failed to
ignite the brush and, barring a scorched or charred spot here
and there, the body was practically untouched.

John Jenkins, of Berrien county, Michigan, located in the
marsh and in the Township of Lake in the year 1865. Shafer
was killed in March of 1869 and in the interim Jenkins had
been elected to the office of Jus- tice-of-the-peace. On
hearing the news of Shafer's death early the following
morning, he proceeded to look up the law to see what his
duties as Justice were in the emergency, there being no
regularly qualified coroner available. He found that the law
provided that the Justice should conduct an inquest in such
cases. Accordingly he repaired to the Shafer home, viewed
the body and took note of the surroundings, and then gave
orders authorizing the removal of the body to his home. Mr.
Jenkins at that time lived on the south-east corner of the
section that adjoins the present village of Lake on the west,

his home being located on the north side of the road about a quarter of a mile from the coroner, west. Situated a little ways to the southeast of his home, Mr. Jenkins had a log black-smith shop where work for the neighborhood was carried on, and to this place the body of "Old Shafer" was directed to be brought. It was late in the afternoon when the body arrived. Two barrels were upended, a wide puncheon slab laid thereon and there, in such state as the limited facilities of the frontier afforded rested the body of the grim old bandit of the marsh in all its wretchedness, still clutching in his left hand the old dish- rag, and with the grime of the day's work up-on him.

Dr. John F. Shronts, who first began the practice of medicine in this swamp region, later moving to Momence, was authorized by Mr. Jenkins to perform an autopsy on the body as the law requires. The day was far spent—in fact it was quite dark by the time Dr. Shronts arrived, so that it became necessary for the Doctor to work by the dim, uncertain light of tallow candles. These were held conveniently by various members of the jury who followed the' Doctor's every move in the gruesome procedure in evident absorption. What a gathering was that of typical frontier types that thronged the little road-side blacksmith shop that night—that last night "Old Shafer" spent this side of the grave! Thrilled by the news of his sudden and tragic demise and that an inquest had been ordered, a most unusual thing for that day, better than a score of Beaver Lake dwellers gathered at the little shop on the roadside, interested spectators of all that went on. Dressed in the rough, weatherworn garb of the hunter and trapper, each one with that indispensable accompaniment of frontier life, a dog or two of the hound species, they surged in and about the place in their eager anxiety to follow every move of the surgeon. Really, Shafer's taking off was an event. The burden of dread under which the community had lived for so many years had thus been suddenly lifted, and that sense of relief experienced by the populace at the passing of so formidable a menace as "Old Shafer" was clearly manifested by a perfect babble of conversation that left no phase of the dead man's life untouched. To the general feeling of security and wellbeing was added, in most cases, a glow of complete satisfaction inspired by generous drinks of whiskey.

Now and then some member of the little company of onlookers that peered through the open door into the yellow-lighted depths of the shop, felt a momentary tremor and a chill in the region of the spine as he beheld the lifeless form, inert and motionless, helpless under the deft, swiftly moving hands of Dr. Shronts. The soft cartilages of the ribs were severed one by one and the sternum entire lifted to an acute angle and nearly two dozen large buck-shot taken from the cavity. The autopsy thus established beyond question or cavil that "Old Shafer" had come to his death from the effects of these buck-shot, fired into his back from a gun in the hands of some person unknown to the jury. There were the buck-shot—a teaspoonful of them—enough to kill three men. And Shafer's neighbors who thus talked of it " 'Lowed thar wuz none too many at that! Just a safe, comfortable load for a man like Mike Shafer—one couldn't be too careful when hunting game like Mike!" At the conclusion of the autopsy the crowd withdrew; one by one the lights were extinguished; the door of the wayside shop was closed and latched and if anyone watched beside that lonely bier that night it was only the invisible spirits of darkness with which he had fraternized in life.

At the Jenkins home across the road the investigation was renewed with a view to dis-covering, if possible, the perpetrator of the crime, although the public, in this instance, did not look upon it as a crime particularly. Two men, Baum and Cushinberry, frequenters of the swamp concerning whose affairs little or nothing was known, were examined. Their stories were conflicting. They admitted having had some dealings with Shafer the day before he was found dead at his cabin. Reluctantly they admitted that they had had a falling out and that Shafer, in his stormy way, had threatened them both with death. Although the two operated much together, there was a notable discrepancy in the testimony they gave concerning their business affairs. Harking back to that night of more than a half century ago, Mr. A. B. Jenkins, now of Morocco, Indiana, then a lad of eleven years, recalls the furtive, shifty manner, in which they gave their testimony and has no hesitancy in pronouncing them the real culprits. They were told to hold themselves in readiness to appear before the jury again next day but, instead, they set out on foot in the darkness for the nearby Illinois state-line. Captain Silas Sink, a resident of the Beaver Lake country, who was returning from Momence late that night, met them only a mile or so east of the state-line. The wives of Baum and Cushinberry, after several months, left the country and joined them in all probability. They were never heard from after that. In the course of time it came out that these men were counterfeiters, working in collusion with Shafer.

THE JOHN JENKINS HOME

*This Place, one-half Mile West of Lake Village, Indiana, was the
Home of John Jenkins in 1865. Here, to the Right in the Picture, stood
a Little Log Blacksmith Shop Where the Autopsy "was Held on the
Remains of "Old Shafer."*

Fred Tanner, a resident of the Beaver Lake country towards whom suspicion pointed an accusing finger, was held to the grand jury as a result of the coroner's jury investigations. It was brought out that there had been a bitter feud between Shafer and Tanner resulting from Tanner having lost several head of colts which he charged Shafer with having fed with poisoned corn. Tanner was emphatic in his charge against Shafer and most persistent in his efforts to make the old outlaw pay for them. So insistent did Tanner become in pressing his claim for the colts that "Old Shafer" was finally driven to the extremity of issuing an ultimatum, the gist of which was something as follows: "I am not going to pay a cent for the horses but, I am going on your trail with a gun at ten o'clock tomorrow, and when I get through with you, your hide wont hold ear corn!" And those who knew anything of Shafer's iron will and implacable spirit, once they were aroused, knew that a statement of that nature from him meant serious trouble if not bloodshed. The trial of Tanner later by the civil authorities resulted in his being acquitted.

Shafer was buried the following morning. There was no semblance of a funeral. Those were primitive days in the Lake country and the deceased inspired merely a sense of relief, now that he was gone. The remains with only the scant covering afforded by the half-burnt clothes he wore the day he was killed, were deposited in the bed of a lumber wagon and conveyed to the little frontier cemetery that now serves the town of Lake Village, two miles away to the north-west, on a high, sandy knoll. Following the wagon as it moved along the sandy trail were eight or ten marsh citizens who had helped to swell the crowd at the autopsy and who were animated by a desire "to see the thing through." Several were on horseback; others walked, and as they walked they smoked and cracked jokes and laughed, while the hounds, ranging the countryside in joyous abandon, added their deep-toned baying to the medley of sounds more joyful than sad the day Shafer went to his long home.

THE LAKE VILLAGE CEMETERY.

This Cemetery is Located Two Miles Northwest of the Village Near This High Spot a Hole Was dug in the Sand and "Old Shafer's Remains Tumbled in Without Coffin or Shroud, While the Throng Joked and Made Merry,

No coffin was provided, not even a rough box of boards. This man who for so long, outraged the laws of God and man, who had murdered his own child and hid her body in the lonely waste with only a covering of sand, deserved nothing better for himself. In fact, the consensus of opinion was that he really did not deserve that much. So, a hole, a shallow one, not a grave exactly, was hastily dug, the remains deposited therein and as hastily covered over. With the last shovelful on the mound the wielder of the shovel raised it high and brought it down with a resounding whack, remarking while the onlookers guffawed: "There you are, Mike Shafer, and may the devil make you dance a hornpipe on the hottest griddle there is in hell."

It is generally believed that the body of Shafer did not long remain in its lonely abode on the very peak of the wind-swept sand knoll. Several days later his grave showed unmistakable signs of having been disturbed. Some said it was the work of the wolves. Others guessed shrewdly that it was the work of a younger set of boys who had avowed their intention of stringing the body of Shafer up to a jack-oak tree. Mr. Jenkins is of the opinion that the skeleton of a body which the devil would not have claimed would, never-the-less, have been hailed as a valued accessory to a doctor's outfit in that day of the frontier. Various rumors were rife concerning the final disposition of the body. He says imagination might picture a fire burning under a capacious old fashioned soap-kettle, set in some convenient copse of scrub-oak secure from prying eyes, wherein the body of the old bandit was gradually reduced, and not be far off the truth, possibly. And in that case, what could be more fitting as a finale to a life of crime than those well-known lines from Macbeth, where the witches chant—

"Double, double toil and trouble, Fire burn and cauldon bubble!"

JOHN HADDON MAKES A KILLING

John Haddon was, for years well known in and about Momence as a hunter, trapper and all around frontiersman. He was a character whose oddities are still recalled by some of the older residents. He was the last of the picturesque wilderness types that served the sparse settlements of the prairie as mail carrier. When the Illinois Central built into Kankakee in 18-53, Haddon lost his job. Prior to 1841 Momence citizens used to go to Chicago or Bunkum for their mail. When Mo-mence got a post office finally, in 1841 it is said, the mail was brought from Baileytown, Indiana, ten miles west of Michigan City, to Momence and Bourbonnais, by Oliver Warner. This route did not last long, evidently. Most of the old timers remember Heber Rexford who carried the mail on his back from Chicago to old Bunkum by way of the Chicago- Vincennes Trail. Anselem Chipman succeeded Rexford on the mail route and Haddon followed Chipman.

Mr. R. A. Hewitt recalls the story of Haddon and the deer as related by the late James S. Garrett. After losing his job as carrier of the mail, Haddon, in the early fifties, like many other of the early settlers about Momence, spent a portion of the winter months in the timber along the Kankakee river east of Momence getting out logs, which were floated down to the saw-mill. Momence for a time, it is said, had the only saw-mill on the river between Wilmington and the Indiana state-line. It will be remembered by many that the remains of the old mill were still standing at late as 1873.

On one of these winter trips of Haddon's to the timber he discovered a goodly herd of deer on one of the small islands nearby. Thinking that fresh venison would be a welcome change from the regulation "pork and beans" of a winter camp, he crossed over to the island on the ice with axe and bowie-knife in hand. The herd, frightened by his approach, made a wild dash for the river. They no sooner struck the ice than they went sprawling in all directions. Haddon, as he pursued them on the ice found himself in pretty much the same predicament, he being shod with boots full of hob-nails in the soles. The deer were helpless and so was he. But, in an instant, he resolved that he would not let a mere matter of hob-nailed boots interfere with a "bag" so valuable as this, so, down on the ice he sat, off came the boots and, like Bobby Burns' witch in Tam O'Shanter, he didn't go after them in his "sark," but in his stockings. He completed the slaughter of the herd, some ten or a dozen, and to his sorrow found that his feet were so badly frozen that it was with great difficulty that he got back to camp.

Just what disposition was ever made of the venison and hides of this herd Mr. Garret was unable to say. Perhaps it was distributed among the numerous camps on the upper river after reserving a goodly portion for Haddon himself as he lingered in camp nursing a pair of badly frozen feet.

It is related of Haddon that one day when Yankee Robinson's show exhibited in Momence, he attended. Clad in his unique frontiers garb of buckskin shirt and coon-skin cap Haddon was leaning against one of the poles that supported the top, when a circus employee spoke to him rather roughly and told him to get out of there. Haddon paid no attention to the fellow and again he yelled: "Say, you, get away from that pole and be damn quick about it." Haddon reached for his hunting knife with the remark: "You clear out of here yourself or I'll open you from end to end like a herrin'." And Haddon continued to lean against that pole until he became so weary he just had to sit down.

Haddon always maintained that he had Indian blood in his veins and something of color was given to the statement by reason of his dark and swarthy countenance. For years, after the customs of developing civilization had gradually displaced those of the frontier, Haddon continued to wear the buckskin hunting shirt and coon-skin cap, and al-ways at his side dangled the hunting knife of the woodsman. The old ferry that used to be operated in an early day west of the island-point at Momence, had, on each side of the river, great hewn white-oak posts set in the ground to which the ferry cable was made fast. Haddon, at some time, appropriated the post on the south side of the river and removed it to his farm (which later was owned by R. A. Hewitt), where, after all these years, it is still, in use. Mr. Hewitt tells that he dug it out, cut off a portion of it and re-set it to do duty as a gate-post.

"CHIEF WHITE FOOT" VISITS HIS BIRTH PLACE

Mrs. Orra F. Allen, of Momence, has kindly furnished us the following incident concerning the old Pottawattomie chief "White Foot."

In the year 1872 my father, Lewellyn H. Foster, and family, lived on a farm north and west of Momence, known as the Huntley farm. On a very hot day in the early spring of that year, we children, who were playing together in the yard, were very much surprised on beholding an exceptionally large Indian and his squaw and two children coming into the yard. We children flew for the house and mother's protecting arms.

The big Indian gave his name as "Chief White Foot," a Pottawattomie of the Prairie Band who, years before, when this was the domain of his people, had been born near unto where our home stood. He asked permission to pitch his camp for the night in the yard, which permission was readily granted. They remained for a portion of the following day, during which time "White Foot" silently surveyed the surroundings of the land of his birth with evident satisfaction. Late in the afternoon they resumed their journey. Their objective was Beaver Lake, where they spent the summer. The Beaver Lake country, in that day, was a wonderful retreat for wild game.

It is recalled that, upon their return in the early fall, it was quite cold. Again they asked permission to pitch their tepee in the yard. On this occasion, in the course of conversation, "White Foot" proudly exhibited his bare feet, one of which, by some rare freak of nature, was much whiter than the other hence, the title "White Foot." The old chief was especially proud of his two sons and, on the other hand, was mean to his squaw, all of which was deeply impressed on the youthful minds of the children of our family.

Chief White Foot was a very large Indian, and presented a very stunning appearance rigged in his Indian paraphernalia. He wore moccasins, a brilliantly colored blanket, and a very queer head-gear made up of beautiful eagle feathers and others of many colors. I remember my mother saying, after they had gone, that these colored feathers were from a very rare bird, rare even in that day. The squaw wore very large ear-rings of hammer ed silver, besides a quantity of beads, while her fingers were ornamented with large, showy rings of brass. She also wore a metal circlet on her ankle. The squaw, also, wore a bright colored blanket which completely enveloped her ample form. She wore nothing on her head and neither did the sons. When they departed Chief White Foot gave to mother a beaded buckskin bag which is still preserved as a prized memento of the old days. To my younger sister he gave a pair of beaded moccasins.

This was the last ever seen of White Foot and his family in this neighborhood and the date 1872 probably marks the last of the hunting parties of the Pottawattomi of the west, seeking the old haunts of their people on the Kankakee and over in the Indiana marshes.

REMINISCENCES OF W. W. PARISH, SENIOR

The following interesting reminiscences of one of Momence's oldest and most popular citizens were happily collated by Hon. C. M. C. Buntain while Mr. Parish was at his best, and were published in the Momence Progress of December 27, 1912. These reminiscences fit in perfectly and form a most valuable contribution to the lore of early days in Kankakee county which it is the purpose of this volume to preserve. Mr. Parish's varied activities, his rise to affluence by means of frugality and industry, should prove an inspiration to the youth of today, who enjoy advantages and opportunities undreamed of in the days when Mr. Parish came into the west. His story follows.

"In 1840, in September, I left home in Naples, N. Y. for the west. I first drove overland eighteen miles to Canandaigua, our county-seat then, by the so-called "strap railroad" to Rochester, then by the Erie Canal to Buffalo, thence by boat to Chicago. This boat had no regular schedule. At Chicago or Milwaukee there was then no harbor. We were landed by lighter. A small boat would come out to the steamer and received the passengers and the cargo. Chicago at this time was a small country village. I went overland from Chicago to Momence; stopped at a place on the "Sac Trail," called a hotel, about three miles south of Crete, but which was nothing more nor less than one of the old Pennsylvania wagon boxes. This hotel was kept by Mr. Brown. Later a substantial log house was substituted for the wagon-box hotel, and still later a frame house took its place.

It will be remembered that the "Sac Trail" was an old Indian trail running from Detroit to St. Louis. When I reached

Momence, after a continuous trip of eighteen days, I found but one log house situated on the west side of what is now known as Range street, near the present site of Burdick & Joubert's drug store. I hired out to A. S. Vail and Orson Beebe at fifty cents a day. As there were no stores in the village our trading point for groceries, in fact everything, was Chicago. When we secured a mill on the Kankakee river then we had our rough lumber, but still had to haul all finishing lumber from Chicago. I have seen as many as two hundred wagons at one time camping on the river banks at Momence enroute to Chicago. Cattle and hogs were driven to Chicago from as far south as Vermilion county, Illinois. I distinctly remember of seeing a drove of five hundred turkeys being driven to Chicago. They camped on the island in Momence overnight.

My wife and I began keeping house with the sum of sixty dollars. With my ox team and money, constituting all our property, we drove to Chicago for our household furniture. There were no homes between Momence and Goodenow. Returning with the furniture, our wagon was mired in the mud and sloughs, near what is now Harvey, Illinois. I carried my wife out of the wagon and then the groceries and furniture, and with the aid of a log chain the oxen succeeded in drawing the empty wagon out of the almost impassable road. It took us one week to make the trip. Settled in our log house near Momence, in a new country, I began the only occupation at that time, apparently, open to man—farming. Our tools were all hand-made, and we made them. They consisted of a wooden plow, a wooden drag and a hand-sickle, and later, a cradle took its place. Our threshing floor was on the prairie. Oxen stamped out the grain and the wind separated the chaff from the wheat. Nature's threshing machine gave way to what was called a "Hedge-Hog" machine.

During the period from 1840 to 1850, you had the choice of farm lands for $1.25 per acre. Wheat delivered in Chicago was worth 35 cents a bushel; dressed pork, $1.50 per hundred; corn and oats, ten cents per bushel. I distinctly remember of giving 700 bushels of oats and corn mixed for an old horse, the first I ever owned. The first wheat I ever saw was in 1841. It was growing on a tract of land immediately east of the Chicago-Vincennes State Road, on the William (Squire) Nichols farm, east of the brick house (now standing) and east of the Chicago-Vincennes Road at the point marked by the stone "179." I helped to cut all this wheat with a hand sickle at fifty cents a day. The wheat yielded forty bushels an acre, and the market price was 35 cents a bushel.

As soon as the Illinois Central was built through the county, the price of land advanced to $7 per acre, according to the distance from the railroad. Land values from this time gradually increased, and during the civil war I owned eighty acres of what is now occupied by the dwelling houses on the south side of the river, at Momence, and east of the

Chicago & Eastern Illinois Railroad. This tract was worth about forty or fifty dollars an acre. I sold wheat from this land that yielded thirty-five bushels to the acre, for which I received $2.20 per bushel at the Momence mill. The land adjoining this tract, now owned by my son, is worth according to present values (1912), $200 per acre. Eighty acres of land in the Six-Mile Grove, near Momence, where the Nichols cemetery is now located, was traded to William

(Squire) Nichols for a span of mules. Prior to this mill we drove to Attica, Indiana, a distance of seventy- five miles, to have our wheat ground. This lasted but one year. Then we drove to Wilmington, Illinois, a distance of thirty miles, for our flour. This continued for a number of years.

The first corn I ever saw planted was by the father of Andrew Dayton, east of Momence. His wife dropped the corn and he pushed the dirt over it with his foot. The first corn planter was a hand-jabber, planting two rows at a time. Mr. John Wicks, of Momence, sold them. We drove twenty-five miles south of Momence to get our mail, and received it once a week. The manuscript was folded and sealed with a wafer. It took two months for a letter mailed in Naples, N. Y., to reach Momence. The postage was twenty- five cents, paid by the receiver. Lorain Beebe was the first postmaster at Momence. The Kankakee river was the dividing line between Will and Iroquois counties, south of the river being Iroquois county and Will (now Kankakee) county on the north. The county-seat of Iroquois county was Middleport, one mile west of what is now Watseka, on the Iroquois river. I frequently served as juror in the circuit court there. Court would not last over a week or two. I heard Abraham Lincoln try a lawsuit there in 1840 or 1841. He came up from Danville on horseback. We used to gather around him and hear him tell his stories. I might say, in passing, that the next time I saw him was in his own home in Springfield, where I shook hands with him, the year he was nominated for the presidency. I was in Springfield for two days. He had a pile of rails in his back yard and before I came away they were all taken by the relic hunters.

John Chamberlain, John Wertz and myself were elected three "Side Judges" of Iroquois county. Our duties were similar to those of the supervisors now. The county was badly in debt. Its debts were paid by county orders, and men bought these at fifty cents on the dollar and paid their taxes with them. We three decided to stop this, and by our efforts made them worth par. We then got some money, and the first thing we did was to put a roof on the court house. My colleagues were opposed to the carving out of Kankakee county from Iroquois and Will, and strenuously worked to retain the old boundaries, as I did for the new. The people by their votes settled the matter in a way satisfactory to me. It was a day's journey to the Middleport county-seat. Lawyers from Joliet rode horseback to Middleport to try cases, and Iroquois county lawyers rode to Joliet for the same purpose. My first tax receipt was for fifteen cents, being the taxes on my sole property, a yoke of oxen. At this time the sheriff collected the taxes. They were paid to him on the old Lowe farm, near the present East Court street bridge over the Kankakee river. An overland trip to Joliet was a day's journey, the first stage being as far as Coon Grove, near Goodenow, the second stage the Twelve-Mile Grove, (twelve miles from Joliet), and the third stage the Five- Mile Grove. This was the route in dry roads and weather. In wet times, we traveled by the way of Bourbonnais—the first stage being at the tavern of Uncle Tommy Durham, at Bourbonnais, and the next at Wilmington.

During the sixties we were greatly bothered by horse thieves. We organized an Anti- Horse Thief Association. We found that within a short time fifteen horses had been stolen within our immediate neighborhood. A nice span of grays were stolen one night from the barn of Zeno Brayton. I was delegated to hunt down the thief. Enlisting Hannibal Worcester, we drove to Crown Point, Ind., and traced the thief to Chicago, and found him and the horses five miles west of Chicago. I knew the team as soon as I saw them, arrested the thief, sold my horse, hitched one of the grays to the buggy and led the other. The friends at Momence knew we were coming and one hundred of them met us at Tower Creek, near the present Lankow farm, two miles west of Momence, on the Kankakee river, and wanted to hang the thief. We were bringing him to Momence for trial before a justice-of-the-peace. Russel Seager prevailed upon the crowd not to hang him, and they desisted. We brought him to Momence from whence the sheriff took him to Kankakee. Later, he was indicted and made his escape from jail. We received from this thief five horses and colts belonging to Dick Griswold, and a saddle horse belonging to John Wickes. Our trip covered a period of four days.

I attended the convention at Chicago that nominated Abraham Lincoln for the presidency; was too poor to travel to hear the Lincoln-Douglas debates. I 'heard Stephen A. Douglas speak at the Court House in Kankakee, during the presidential campaign. Knew him well. I was born and brought up a democrat, but voted the Republican ticket, beginning with President Polk, up to the present time."

THE OLD LOG HOUSE

This log house was built by Cornelius Cane for a residence in 1838, and was located about two and a half miles north-east of Momence. The first election held in the county was held in this log house in 1840. Mr. William Nichols was elected Squire. John Cane, son of Cornelius Cane, was elected constable, and at the some election William Henry Harrison, grandfather of Benjamin Harrison, was elected president of the United States. The campaign procession was led by two violins, played by James and Nelson Graham, brothers of Mrs. Fred Knighthart, of Momence. Thomas Grimes was marshal of the day on the Whig side. When W. W. Parish came to Illinois, he boarded with Mr. Cane, paying $1.25 per week for his board. They had corn dodger six days in the week, and biscuits and "chicken fixin's" on Sunday. Mr. Cane always asked the same blessing, which was as follows: "Oh, Lord, we praise thee for the present refreshments; pardon our sins, give us grace and wisdom, that we may have the profits we gain thereby, for Jesus' sake— John, pass the corn dodger!"

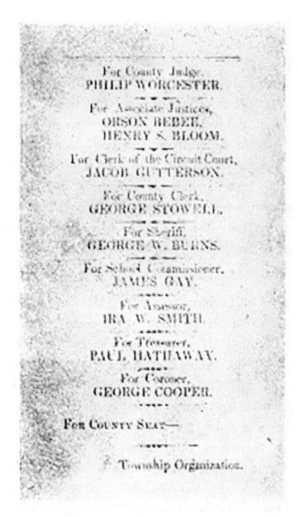

For County Judge.
PHILIP WORCESTER.

For Associate Justices,
ORSON BEBEE.
HENRY S. BLOOM.

For Clerk of the Circuit Court,
JACOB GUTTERSON.

For County Clerk,
GEORGE STOWELL.

For Sheriff,
GEORGE W. BURNS.

For School Commissioner,
JAMES GAY.

For Assessor,
IRA W. SMITH.

For Treasurer,
PAUL HATHAWAY.

For Coroner,
GEORGE COOPER.

For County Seat—

Township Organization.

KANKAKEE COUNTY'S FIRST BALLOT

Kankakee County was Organized in 1863. The Accompanying Engraving Shows the First Printed Ballot at the First Election for County Officers, June 21, 1853. The Location of the County Seat was Determined at This Election, Momence Being Defeated by "Kankakee Depot," as the City was Then Known. This Ballot was Found Among the Effects of the Late Henry S. Bloom.

141

MEMORIES OF THE OLD HILL BRIDGE

Mrs. Argale Nichols, of Kankakee, still hale and hearty at ninety, was the eldest daughter of James Graham who came with his family from Indiana to the neighborhood of Momence, in the year 1838. The pioneer home of the Grahams was on the north side of the Kankakee river, near to the Chicago- Vincennes Trail, and not very far from famous Hill Tavern which, however, was located on the south bank of the river. Sometime in the early forties, it may have been 1842, the first bridge was built over the Kankakee, on the line of the Chicago-Vincennes Road, near to where the Hill Tavern was located.

She was a girl of seven or eight years at the time and her chief delight was to sit on the bank of the river and watch the efforts of Bonnie E. Boardman, as he scored and hewed and framed the heavy timbers. Boardman, she says, was the architect and chief workman on the old Hill bridge. The ford at this point on the trail was one of the finest and most practical on the river. The bed of the Kankakee here had many large, flat stones, disposed so that the road was fairly smooth. In the very early days this was a favorite spot for the Pottawattomi to come and spear fish. During those early days of her childhood, she says, the Kankakee was literally swarming with the finest fish, and often she turned her attention from the workmen scoring timbers to the river's crystal flood to behold the hordes of bass, pickerel, red-horse and sturgeon moving majestically head-on against the stream.

Beaver Lake and the Kankakee swamps to the north-east, in that day, were the natural hatcheries for fish. Such another natural habitat for fish and wild fowl as the swamp region of the Kankakee, was never surpassed anywhere in the United States.

After the timbers had been hewed and framed, the word was sent out that there was to be a "grand raisin'." Settlers from far and near responded in numbers and gave liberally of their time and labor. Mr. Peter Strickler, of Iroquois, who died recently at the ripe age of 95, was present on this occasion and helped. It was a jolly time, enlivened by generous feeds, a la pioneer, at the tavern. Between times there was plenty to drink, for whiskey in that day was not only plentiful but cheap. One could buy a gallon for twenty-five cents.

During the years in which they lived on the Chicago-Vincennes Trail many were the Indians that visited them during the early spring and summer. The squaws had strings of beads and other articles of bead work, which they offered for sale together with articles of wearing apparel made of buckskin. Many of these nomadic visitors, in time, became well known to the members of the Graham family, enough so that they often called them by name. They were friendly, kindly, a little obtrusive at times perhaps, but, on the whole, the recollection, after all these years, reverts to them with feelings of genuine pleasure.

Apples and other fruits raised by the Indiana farmers were readily obtained by the pioneer families living on the Chicago-Vincennes Trail, for this was the great highway over which much of this produce was hauled. Mrs. Nichols recalls that her mother used to pare and slice quantities of apples

143

and peaches and then string them on a tape. Long strings of fruit were thus prepared, after which they were festooned about the house to undergo the process of drying. Large quantities of fruit were prepared in this way. The only other method employed was preserving. The idea of canned fruit as we have it in this day, had not been evolved at that time.

THE "GOLL DUMMED" RAILROAD

That innovations stuck "hard" in the crop of the average pioneer there can be no doubt. Grandfather and grandmother William Nichols who established the well-known Nichols home north of Momence, near to the Chicago-Vincennes Trail, in an early day, regarded with considerable suspicion the newfangled ideas of civilization. They were pioneers bred in the bone, who always found the old-time methods sufficient unto their needs. It is related of them that, shortly after the building of the C. D. & V. railroad, now the Chicago & Eastern Illinois, they one day had occasion to cross the railroad track on their way to visit the Grahams. As they drew near the crossing a train, consisting of several antiquated coaches drawn by a wheezy, wood- burning engine, happened along.

Their pioneer souls were thrilled by this most unusual sight and grandmother, in her excitement, grabbed grandfather Nichols by the arm with one hand while she pointed with the other, exclaiming as she did so, "Why, dad drat it, William, there's people a ridin' in them keers!" After the train had passed, they drove cautiously up onto the rails and grandpa stopped squarely astride of them, and watched the spectre retreat until it was well out of sight. At the Grahams that day, grandpa and grandma's unusual experience with the cars was easily the main topic of conversation. This experience may have been enlarged upon somewhat in the course of narration but, if so, they simply made use of a privilege which the world concedes to all who tell of startling things first hand. The railroad with its "keers," easily held the center of the stage that afternoon, and the terrible ravages of the dreaded "milk-sick," over in the Exline woods, was not mentioned once.

In the days of 1840, when "Uncle Bill" Parish came to Momence, the Pottawattomi were still found in numbers occupying tepees in the woods along the Kankakee. Chiefly they were of the band of White Pigeon, intermingled with those who at one time, acknowledged the chieftainship of "Pierre Moran," a Frenchman who was a chief by reason of having married the daughter of a chief. This story told of "Uncle Bill," illustrates his well-known speculative instinct. In that primitive day of the pioneer the fur-bearing animals of the woods were sought industriously by everybody—Indian and white man alike. One day in the winter while traversing the woods east of town, Mr. Parish ran across the trail of a coon in the snow. He followed it for some distance until finally it terminated at a hollow tree. Almost simultaneously there appeared a Pottawattomie Indian in quest of game. "Uncle Bill" was a quick thinker. Pointing to the tracks of the coon in the snow he remarked: "I sell 'em for one dollar," at the same time holding up a finger significantly.

Much to his surprise the Indian replied: "You're on," at least it meant that in effect, for he handed over a dollar. Thus in undisputed possession of the property, the Indian went after it and, by the time he had finished the job, he had taken out four fine coons. Four coon hides at the trader's brought "one plus," which was the equivalent of two dollars, to say nothing of the meat. Mr. Parish said that Indian did so well on that deal that he did not work again for a month.

"UNCLE MARK" ATHERTON AND THE TRAPPERS

In 1851 Marcus A. Atherton came to Mo-mence. As a youth he was employed by F. M. Tompkins, who carried on a small tin shop in the near vicinity of the present tannery on River street. His very first piece of work was that of the spouting and guttering for the Strunk mansion which still lingers amid shadows of giant elms on the bank of the south branch on the island, a ghost of old days, grim and gray, unchanged since the days when Atherton worked on it. In 1853 Mr. Atherton engaged in a general mercantile business which he operated for many years. As a merchant he was distinctly typical of old times and new.

In the old days of the early fifties in and about Momence, the hunter and trapper was a more important element in the trade of the backwoods store than the farmer, although this condition gradually changed as time went on and the country developed from frontier to the civilization of today. The river stretches of the Kankakee and the contiguous marshes afforded an ideal field for the operations of the trapper who sought the smaller fur-bearing animals. Coon, mink, skunk, fox and musk-rat pelts constituted, in a very great measure, the currency of the border among the hardy, picturesque trapper types who frequented the place.

They were, as a rule, a happy-go-lucky improvident lot, whose shacks out in the timber on the river were generally bare of luxuries, yet whose owners lived on the fat of the land, nevertheless. Life's philosophy was summed up in the terse statement: "There will always be a river; there will always be timber; there will always be game to trap; always a little "corn liquor to drink, and a little terbacker to smoke!" What more

147

did a man of the border want? Why worry about a future so full of promise?

"Uncle Mark" Atherton stood "ace high" as the saying goes, with this primitive clientele of the river and the woods. For years he furnished them their supplies when the trapping season was on, extending credit until such a time when the season's catch was brought in. He was a fair man, a square man, who never held out the least iota in the weight of the bacon, corn meal, sugar and tea that went over his scale. The story is told of one man to whom "Uncle Mark" extended credit, who particularly insisted that he was "to take the varmint pelts as they run." "That's all right, said "Uncle Mark" accommodatingly, "I'll take 'em as they run."

The fall and winter passed and, one after, another, the trappers to whom credit had been given dropped in and squared up, all but this particular individual. "Uncle Mark" met him one day and called his attention to the fact that his "credit" was overdue. "But you agreed to take them pelts as they run," said the debtor. "Of course, I did," replied Mr. Atherton, "what's that got to do with the delay in paying?" "Oh, nothin', "drawled the trapper, who was something of a wag, "only they're still a-runnin'."

For the space of a minute or more "Uncle Mark" was swamped with righteous indignation, and then the humor of the situation bore in upon him and he laughed. "That's a hoss on me," he acknowledged; "tell you what I'll do, though; I'll give you credit on exactly the same terms, only I'll close the back door of the store and leave the front door open—you agreein' to shoo them pelts into the place 'as they run.'" The incident caused much amusement among the men of the border populace and cost "Uncle Mark" many and many a drink of "corn whiskey," until it seemed as though the "bar'l" in the back end of the store was in danger of giving out entirely under the long continued strain. The tenacity with which the frontier memory clung to this incident of the border was little short of marvelous.

"NIGGER DOC"

Among the many well-known characters who, at one time or another, figured in the early-day population of Momence, was "Nigger Doc." How he came by the unique title of "Doc," the memory of the oldest inhabitant is at a loss to account for. He was a powerful negro, jet black, of amiable disposition generally whose one great weakness was liquor. He was the butt of many a good natured joke and sally of wit—in short rather indispensable to that class of loungers who amused themselves at the expense of somebody else. Colonel Zeno Brayton, a popular early day business man of Momence, one day gave "Nigger Doc" a broad-brimmed black felt hat he had discarded. "Doc" was delighted with the gift. He made himself conspicuous with the new lid and never missed an opportunity to make known to the various ones he met that "Kunnel Zeno Brayton dun gave it to him." "Doc" was standing one day before the bar of the old saloon that used to stand on the west side of Range street all set to offer a libation to the god of fortune, the libation in this case being nothing less than a generous beer-mug filled to the brim with gin and about whose top "Doc's fingers closed that not one precious drop of the fluid might be lost, when Cal Hayes, a Momence blacksmith, sidled in. Hayes, for reasons best known to himself, had conceived a violent dislike for the black race and for "Nigger Doc" in particular. He had made open threats on various occasions "that he was a going to get Nigger Doc, and get him good." On this occasion as Hayes beheld "Doc" draining the gin from the beer- mug his hand sought his coat pocket and brought forth an old bandana handkerchief, in the corner of which he had tied a stone about the size of a hen's egg. With this formidable implement he blazed away blindly at the negro's head. The blow was a terrific one but, aside from the momentary surprise of the attack, apparently did not feaze "Nigger Doc" for an instant. The assailant made for the back door of the saloon with the negro in pursuit. The back yard of this saloon was surrounded by a high board fence, forming a sort of bull-pen, where many a bout of fisticuffs and boxing had been pulled off in the past. Hayes, more agile than his pursuer, scrambled up and over the barricade like a cat and made his escape. "Doc" sauntered back into the saloon and, taking off the precious hat, showed the crowd a hole in the side of it made by the stone in the sling. High up on his head was a huge welt from which the blood trickled in a stream and, as he looked upon the hat, sorrowfully he ruminated: "Jes' look at dat beau'ful hat dat Kunnel Zeno Brayton dun give me—plum ruined by dat no-'count Cal Hayes."

JOE BARBEE, OF INDIAN GARDEN

Like the opening of a door long unused— like the shifting of a window shade that has long been closely drawn—like a sudden gleam of sunshine revealing the treasures within, so, suddenly, there came to Mrs. Argale Nichols, she who was the eldest daughter of that pioneer settler at the "Upper Crossing," James Graham, recollections of an unique Indian character of her childhood days on the Kankakee, eighty years ago. Mrs. Nichols recalls perfectly that this Indian had a white man's name. He was known as Joe Barbee and his home was located above the Parmlee place on the Kankakee river. He was not an out and out Pottawattomie, but a half breed, whose dash of white blood was noticeable not so much in his physical appearance as in that peculiar bent of mind which led him to observe cleanliness, to speak English fluently, and to follow more or less successfully the occupations of the white man.

Joe Barbee's place on the river was known far and wide among the pioneer settlers as "Indian Garden." It was a well-kept spot adjoining Dan Parmlee's famous "Garden of Eden," wherein vegetables were grown, as well as a limited variety of fruits, such as apples, peaches, grapes and blackberries, which Joe attended to assiduously, thereby deriving great pleasure. Joe Barbee, the "working Indian," was the object of quiet speculation on the part of the people of the countryside and, as may be readily supposed, the subject of many an animated discussion. That he was a freak was the general consensus of opinion, as much of a freak as the "white robin," whose appearance now and then is solemnly affirmed by the naturalist.

Joe Barbee's family consisted of a squaw and two daughters. They were essentially Indian in appearance. Their features were set in the grim, unyielding stoicism so characteristic of the race. They never did smile, says Mrs. Nichols, although Joe Barbee, the father of the girls, contrary to all the traditions of the Indian, would now and then flash a most engaging smile. The family frequently visited the Graham home at the "Upper Crossing" on the Hubbard Trace. Joe generally had quantities of fruit contained in neat willow baskets, while the women offered for sale articles of buckskin, ornamented after the aboriginal manner with beads. Invariably the women of Joe's household wore blankets of white which were ornamented with broad bands of brilliant, dazzling red. But that thing which distinguished them as something separate and apart from the Pottawattomi in general, was the fact that the blankets were CLEAN! Apparently the white trace prevailed to just that extent.

Joe Barbee's efforts and achievements in the horticultural line would constitute a most interesting chapter in the lore of the old days in and about Momence if we but knew of them. We do know however, that his efforts were not confined wholly to "Indian Garden," but extended to an island in the Kankakee river above Shelby, Indiana, where he set out, in an early day, an excellent variety of grapes. The island was subsequently called "Grape Island" and by that name it is known today. Long after Joe Barbee had gone, the settlers on the Kankakee knew of the excellence of the grapes of this particular island, and many and fanciful were the tales that were spun regarding their origin there. The late Stephen R. Moore, on various occasions, called our attention to Grape Island, insisting that the seeds of the species then extant were dropped by the early- day French explorers who navigated the waters of the Kankakee. The theory is plausible enough and Judge Moore may have been right in his assumption. But Joe Barbee, "the working Indian," half white, half Indian, was a wizard with roots, shoots and scions, some of which he planted in the soil of Grape Island where for years they continued to thrive and bear.

The story is recalled by Mr. James Kirby of the day when chief White Pigeon and his band left the Kankakee in charge of government agents for their new home west of the Mississippi, near Council Bluffs, Iowa. "Uncle Sid" Vail and White Pigeon were very friendly and, as an evidence of appreciation of the friendship existing between them, invited the chief to his home, there to partake of dinner. White Pigeon, on this occasion, occupied the place of honor on the right of his host. He wore a towering crest of eagle feathers and further honored the event by wearing his best blanket. During the progress of the meal while "Uncle Sid" was voicing his regret that their friendly relations were so soon to terminate, the old chief suddenly encountered some item in the menu of which his taste did not quite approve. Quite unceremoniously and with as little hesitation as he would have shown had he been at home in his own tepee, he spat the offending morsel into his hand and tossed it carelessly under the table, somewhat to the surprise of the host and the great discomfort of the hostess. White Pigeon was a man of few words and, while it is true that he was an imitator of the white man in many unimportant respects, his table manners could have been improved upon, at least so thought Mrs. Vail. Just what the aboriginal palate balked at in this case is a mystery, unsolved even unto this day.

A PLAGUE OF FROGS

Who is there who has lived in Momence or nearby, who does not recall as having known at some time in his life big, fat, easygoing Ralph Day and his estimable spouse, Susie? Not a one, we dare say. One couldn't help but know Ralph Day, and knowing him, one couldn't help but like him. And Susie? She was a hustling, bustling, ministering spirit of goodness and self-sacrifice among the in-habitants of the old river town of Momence for years, a never-failing angel of mercy and help-fulness at such times when help was most needed. They were a rare couple were Ralph Day and Susie, whose little eccentricities of thought and speech and action endeared them all the more to people of the little river settlement on the Kankakee. While this story concerns more particularly Ralph Day himself, any mention of him which failed to include the sharer of his joys and sorrows, would be regarded as an unpardonable omission.

Ralph Day was a large, fleshy man who weighed, according to best reports, near to three hundred pounds. He was a jovial, good natured man, thus again sustaining the tradition of geniality ascribed to men of avoirdupois generally. He lived on the corner directly opposite the Charles Astle home, west. He used to attend to the work about the Central House bar and, during the extreme hot weather of late June and July and August, he would walk down to the river at such times when the north branch was not too high, and wade in to where the water came to about his waist, then topple over on his back and float— yes, float lik6 a cork on the surface of the stream. Thus borne by the current he would float down opposite his home, several blocks away, regain his footing and walk out. He always deplored the fact that there was no way of floating upstream successfully, and the patrons of the Central House bar used to "rag" him considerably about it.

There was one year when the frogs appeared in such numbers along the Kankakee as to set the "old-timers" all agog. None of them could recall a similar phenomenon in all the river's history. These frogs were so numerous in places that it was possible to literally shovel them. Ralph, one day, burst into the bar-room breathless with excitement and exclaimed: "There's ten million frogs on the river between my house and the head of the island!" You oughta hear 'em—its a regular frog camp-meetin'." Charley Brassard, he who was familiarly known as "Bluch," was sitting in an arm-chair with his feet comfortably disposed on the sill of one of the front windows. He looked up as Day made the statement and remarked: "Say, Ralph, old kid, you're crazy. There ain't that many frogs in the world, pos-i-tively."

"Yes they is, Bluch," persisted Ralph, "and I ain't crazy, neither!"

"Yes you are," insisted Bluch, "you're, crazier'n a bat. You talk like a child. There ain't a million frogs on the whole river and I got twenty dollars that says so."

"Well, anyhow, I may be crazy, but I ain't no damn fool; and I'll jes' go you twenty that I kin get ten thousand of them by tomorrer mornin'," replied Ralph defiantly.

"I gotya," said Bluch; "put up and get out and hustle them frogs. And don't forget, I'll be lookin' for you!"

Fred Knighthart was appealed to by Ralph to put up the money and, as he handed it over, the act was accompanied by a little advice on the side, gratis, as follows: "Ralph, you'd better apologize to Bluch and ask his pardon, and save the twenty." But Day had his fighting blood aroused. "What! Me 'pologize to him? I will like 'el! Lissen to me— Gettin' them ten thousand frogs is jest as easy as stealin' corn from a blind sow! I know what I'm doin'," said he ominously, whereat everybody roared.

This novel bet was the talk of the place for the remainder of the day and a good bit of the night, and many of Ralph's friends who had laughed at the incident, secretly resolved to be on hand on the morrow and witness the outcome. The following morning Bluch Brassard, calm and imperturable, occupied his accustomed place by the window. He, of all the assembled throng, seemed least interested in the affair as he sat there gazing through the narrow slit in the wall that looked out upon Range street, now the "Dixie." And the crowd waited in pleasurable anticipation of "a scene," at such a time as Ralph did appear. There was going to be some fun, frogs or no frogs.

It was nearing ten o'clock that morning when Ralph Day appeared. He drove a horse hitched to the shafts of a light wagon. There was a barrel in the wagon with a gunny-sack spread over its top, which hardly sufficed to muffle the mighty anvil chorus chant of its occupants. There was a disquieting gritting of "frog's teeth" that made the cold chills gallop up and down Bluch Brassard's back. Ralph Day's rotund face shone like a full harvest moon. There was victory written all over it. He had hardly stopped in front of the hotel when he roared: "Here's yer swamp canaries, Bluch, ol' man; come and get 'em!" But Bluch never moved. "How do I know you've got ten thousand of 'em there?" he said at last.

"Count 'em, count 'em,—you kin count can't yuh?"

And then for a moment Ralph Day, in answer to numerous inquiries from those gathered about the wagon, explained radiantly that "there was just oodles upon oodles of frogs on the river—more'n ten hundred million of 'em—shoveled 'em up in the early mornin'—could have got a million as easy as ten thousand, barrin' the shovelin'." During this animated recital Bluch Brassard never batted an eye. "Want me to set 'em in yer lap so's you kin count 'em handy? interrogated Ralph.

"Take 'em away," said Bluch curtly; "you win!"

"Ain't yuh goin' t' look at 'em, Bluch," persisted Ralph, "after I've gone to all this trouble? The bar'l is mor'n half full! Lord

Amighty, they's never been a bunch of frogs like this in town before—not since them sawmill frogs used to come from up-river and take over the town! Goin' to take the word of a crazy man that they's ten thousand of 'em, eh?"

But Bluch only murmured: "Take 'em away! Take 'em away!" Then, turning his head in the direction of the bar, he met the questioning gaze of the bar-tender squarely and, by an almost imperceptible nod, flashed a message which, liberally interpreted, read: "Give Day the money and give the boys whatever they like, as often as they like, and put the whole thing on one check."

MAFFETT TELLS A "TALL ONE"

Imagination, cleverness and ready wit are qualities that have inured to the more fortunate of mankind in all walks of life, ever since the world began. These qualities are variously employed according to the inclination and temperament of the individual. To illustrate—Charles Maffett, an early-day resident of Kankakee County living between Kankakee and Momence, was widely recognized as a teller of stories which were interesting, clever, amusing, "gripping," in addition to being well told. Maffett could tell a "tall one" in a most convincing way. They were lies— but harmless lies—in the main. Maffett's stories always "went over big," and many a bucolic youth, after having heard him tell one, charged his memory with the subject matter and later sought the glory of the limelight by repeating it as a product of his own. Charles Maffett was a large man weighing right around two hundred and seventy-five pounds. He had a pink and white complexion and was rotund to the point of obesity. He was a slow, deliberate speaker, and rarely ever forgot himself so far as to laugh at one of his own stories, which is evidence indisputable of the finished artist.

The story which he sprung on "Uncle Bill" Parish, of Momence, is still designated among the old-timers as a "Maffett Masterpiece." They met one day on the road to Momence, exchanged greetings as they passed when, all at once, "Uncle Bill" pulled up his horses and called out: "Say, Maffett—tell me the biggest lie you ever heard tell of!"

Maffett thus appealed to, stopped his team and replied somewhat hurriedly: "You'll have to excuse me this mornin', Bill. Really, I'm in an awful hurry. You know, old Elias

Garrett dropped dead last night, and I've been up all night helpin' around, and I'm on my way to Deerson's now to get a coffin for him. Good Mornin'—giddap," and he clucked to his team. He kept on his way deaf to all importunities of "Uncle Bill" who sought to gain full particulars concerning the demise of his neighbor, Garrett. "Uncle Bill" was shocked, taken off his feet completely by the startling news. He hurried home and told his wife who hurriedly patted her hair, slipped on her bonnet, and together the two set out for the Garrett home, sad of heart, appalled at the suddenness with which death strikes. As they approached the Garrett residence they looked for some outward sign of the visitation of the dread reaper. There was none. Judged from outside appearances it was a perfectly normal country household. There was no one moving about—inside or out—no teams hitched to the hitching posts, not a single saddle-horse visible, at which they marveled somewhat. Quietly they drove into the yard; slowly, and with as little show of unbecoming haste as possible, they alighted from the vehicle and made their way slowly towards the house when, suddenly, from the direction of the barnyard, they were accosted by a hearty, cheerful "Halloo there, folks—good mornin' to you!"

It was the corpse himself, hale, hearty and smiling who strode up to them and extended his hand in a greeting which would have shamed the most able-bodied ghost that ever was. Ma Parish was speechless, dumbfounded, utterly undone. "Uncle Bill" was nervous, squeamish, decidedly upset at this unexpected denouement. Like a flash it came to him how he had been victimized by the wiley Maffett who, at his earnest solicitation, had obligingly responded with "the biggest lie" that anybody ever heard tell of.

160

Mrs. Parish looked at Elias Garrett and then at her husband with questioning eyes, and he, like a good sport, who finds it necessary at times to lay his cards face-up on the table, told the story of his meeting with Maffett, and that he had been the innocent dupe of his craftiness. There was a big laugh all around and, apparently, "the corpse" enjoyed the situation much more than did "Uncle Bill" judging from the noise he made. As they were about to leave, Mr. Garrett remarked: "Now, look here, Bill, when I do kick off for sure, I'm going to have word of it carried to you by somebody else 'sides Maffett, for I am fearful you would not believe him under any circumstances now." And at that Mrs. Parish looked upon her husband pityingly and was moved to say: "William, I sometimes doubt the wisdom of my letting you go all alone out on the road and over to Momence among those awful men. You are so simple, so trusting, so gullible—there's no telling where we may be trapseing to next!"

THE ELDERS' CLUB

A good many years back in the history of Momence, there was a select and distinguished coterie made up of the older men of the little community who, in order to relieve the tedium of hours not too fully occupied with the weighty affairs of life, organized a Club where they gathered daily and smoked, and spun yarns, and enjoyed themselves and each other generally. Here all weighty questions of public or personal portent were discussed and threshed out and finally disposed of. Here, too, it often happened that they wooed the Goddess of chance and fortune, that particular deity which is said to preside over the destinies of the game known as "Poker." The way these old boys camped on the trail of this particular Goddess was something little short of scandalous. If ever there was an overworked Goddess, this titular deity of fortune that hung about the outskirts of the Club was it. You would be shocked if we were to spill the names of these old-time boys! It would make the goose-flesh stand out all over you! In order to avoid an epidemic of "goose-flesh," however, we have, on second thought, decided not to tell. We merely allude to them as "the Elders," hence, you may speculate to your heart's content.

There were times when these old boys would sit all day and until far into the night around the big table, when the game ran strong and the spirit of man waxed stubborn and unyielding and he sought the out of doors only after he had "been mopped up clean." Among the company of elders was a suave, mild-mannered type of man, of whom it is said that often he would run amuck with nothing more than a pair of deuces. After throwing a scare into the company, he would quietly gather in his cards and slip them into the deck and when importuned to tell just what he held, replied invariably in a voice that was melody itself, "no man knoweth unto this day!"

There is a tradition that once, from the neighboring city of Kankakee, there came a trio of artists with "the spots," who sought the seclusion of this very club and did then and there stake their worldly goods against those of the elders of Momence. It was some tussle! For five days and nights they "sat," this youthful trio from Kankakee and the elders of Momence. Meals were. brought in, drinks and smokes likewise, and the unceasing battle of the wits and the cards went on. Youth is buoyed up with confidence, exotic, luxuriant; old age fortifies itself with caution and experience! In the end caution and experience prevailed. The elders of Momence praised the work of the youthful trio from Kankakee, bought them tickets via the railroad and sent them home to their folks with the parting assurance that they would be glad to see them any time when they happened to be "in that neck o' the woods."

We have been told on the "quiet" that Hoag was sent for with his dray to move the coin from the Club over to the bank, so great was the haul of treasure. In the interim, while the elders were recovering from the effects of this protracted session, it happened that, one day, one of them drew from his pocket, a handful of loaf sugar squares which he distributed to those who sat about the big circular table. He then propounded this novel scheme:

"Every fellow chips a quarter of a dollar into the "pot." Place your cube of sugar on the table before you and watch it closely! The fellow on whose square of sugar a fly lights first takes the "pot!" The new idea was a "hit" right from the start, and the lowly, pestiferous fly, heretofore banned and shunned by mankind generally was acclaimed with joyous shouts in this stronghold of the elders. Nowhere else in the world would this pastime of the "sugar and the fly" been thought of and adopted so spontaneously.

Some years ago, Momence had a rather nifty baseball club whose work was the pride of the town. Many and many a time they brought home the bacon after a hard, and grueling struggle. The elders were "for them" and risked their piasters on them and increased their store thereby many fold. On one occasion when the club went to Watseka, Illinois, for a game, several of the elders went with them. They took the members of the club to the Iroquois House for dinner. When the elders elected to do anything, they did it right. The day was exceedingly hot and the elders, with their coats off, led the way to the dining room. Greatly to their surprise they were confronted by the head waiter, who informed them that they could not be permitted to sit down at the tables unless they put on their coats. The boys put theirs on but the elders were obdurate—they'd be eternally damned if they would. The situation was embarrassing. The waiter was obliging and offered to rustle a linen duster or two, as a means of getting around the difficulty. But, already the spirit of American independence had boiled over and the fat was in the fire.

"Come on, boys," said one, "we'll go over to Uncle Bill William's tavern, by gad."

And at that, the contingent, twelve to fifteen strong, headed out of the Iroquois House onto the T. P. & W. track and hoofed it two full blocks away to the Williams House. The old Williams House had a reputation second to none in its day, and Uncle Bill, as a Boniface, was never surpassed for genuine quality in old days or new. He was a pioneer of pioneers who ranged his own dining room in shirt sleeves and with his trousers stuffed into the tops of his cowhide boots. The only concession he ever made to fastidious public sentiment was when, on passing through the room where his guests were seated at their meal, he seized the top of his hat with a firm grip and slid it over to an angle of about thirty-two degrees, as if to say "this much I do and no more!" Here our friends were genuinely welcomed and were permitted to appear in hot weather negligee, and no questions asked. And as the elders dallied with their meal, between bites they chuckled raucously and delightedly at the discomfiture of the head waiter at the Iroquois, who was so insistent on clothes at a time when clothes were a positive burden.

CHARLES MAFFETT'S WOODEN STOVE

Sometime during the sixties there appeared one day at East avenue and Court Street, in the City of Kankakee, where the Legris Brothers' bank now it, a man with a curious creation in the way of a stove with a wooden jacket. The stove was thus displayed that the public might give it "the up and down" and "the once over," and at the same time learn of its manifold advantages as set forth by its owner and manufacturer, Mr. Charles Maffett, Esq. The very novelty of the thing enlisted public interest in a day when stoves lacked, generally, much of the perfection attained in this day. A day or so later, Charles Maffett himself, appeared with the new invention on the streets of Momence. Mr. A. B. Jenkins, now of Morocco, Indiana, as a boy, recalls the incident and Maffett's slogan, viz: "A pound of hay will feed ten men!" The stove was viewed by hundreds of people, some few of whom doubtfully acknowledged that it had merit, while the greater number look- upon the maple-wood box, said to be a stove, as the product of a brain seized with a mild and harmless dementia. The truth is, the originator of this stove, an old man and a floater whom Maffett had taken pity on and given asylum in his own home, instead of being demented was, in reality, so far in advance of his time that he had the idea of the "fireless cooker" all but perfected. This product of the old inventor's brain was, after all, merely a wooden box supplied with an inner compartment or double lining of tin of sufficient capacity to hold a gallon or so of water. This water was previously heated and poured into the compartment and, in order that the water might be kept hot, there was provided at one side, a small fire-box where a fire of chips could be kept going. We are told that this device, popularly dubbed "the wooden stove," cooked many articles popular in the culinary economy of that day and did it beautifully. Apparently, there was no question as to the excellence of the products turned out by the wooden stove, but, for all that, the purchasing public of Kankakee and Momence was wary and cautious to a degree that rendered its sales almost nil.

A few, however, more courageous than the rest, bought stoves and used them successfully. We wish it were possible to give the reader some sort of description of this early- day innovation in stoves. Unfortunately there is no cut or picture of it extant. Mr. Charles Sherman and the late John Plummer, both old-time residents of Kankakee, recall perfectly the advent of Maffett's wooden stove, each witnessed public demonstrations of it, but neither could recall its structure other than that it was a box-like affair sup-plied with a water compartment of tin. The thermos bottle and the fireless cooker are indispensable adjuncts of almost every home in this day of the twentieth century. The late Elbert Hubbard, speaking of the scientific developments of the century which have contributed most to the comfort and pleasure of living, reckons the development of the thermos principle as among the greatest.

How strange that an old man, homeless, friendless, wandering up and down the world without a dollar, should have touched, in his peripatetic exile, upon an idea so pregnant with possibilities! Strange, indeed, that his idea of half a century ago, should have approximated in its important details, the fire- less cooker of today. Strange, too, was the insistent idea of the inventor, when seeking for a name for this new creation, to call it a stove. The public of that day could not reconcile the idea of a stove that was worthwhile, with a mere box of wood lined with tin. Stoves, as the public regarded them, were constructed of iron and never of wood. This stove of Maffett's therefore, lacked in the elements of successful construction. Ideas are stubborn things and hard to combat. Though the products of the wooden stove were excellent be-yond any question, still, the public had its doubts; at all events it was unconvinced, and such as were

"convinced against their will, were of the same opinion still!"

Messrs. Mateer & Scovill who, at that time, operated the Kankakee planing mill, were deeply interested in this novel invention, and, after having made numerous experiments with it, entered into negotiations with Maffett for the right to manufacture and sell the stove. It is said that they secured the rights to sell the same in the state of California. This stove was supplied with a high-sounding, flamboyant title which, unfortunately, did not long survive and is therefore lost to us in this day. The venture of Messrs. Mateer & Scovill, sad to say, did not prove a success, largely for the reason that Californians were just as skeptical, bone-headed and perverse as the "Suckers" of Illinois. Apparently, all this invention needed to put it over, was an up-to-date demonstrator and advertising man of the twentieth century type.

KANKAKEE COUNTY'S FIRST SCHOOL TEACHER

Kankakee county's first school teacher was an energetic, vivacious little Miss of tender years, comparatively, who accompanied the families of A. S. Vail and Orson Beebe to the banks of the Kankakee in the year 1836. She was Miss Lorain Beebe, sister of Orson Beebe and Mrs. A. S. Vail. While the others set themselves to the task of building a home in the virgin wilderness, Miss Beebe helped her sister keep house and devoted part of her time to teaching school. This first school was held in a room of Asher Sargeant's cabin, the first human habitation built on the site of Momence, and was opened in the winter of 1837. This first school teacher in the first school in Kankakee county, had two pupils. They were the children of Asher Sargeant, who thus shares honors with Miss Beebe in the matter of inaugurating education in the wilderness in that he furnished the school house and the pupils. This first attempt at school teaching was subject to interruptions on account of the weather. She taught only three hours a day and only on such days when she was enabled to cross the Kankakee on the ice. The school curriculum of that day embraced only the "three R's," and they were enough. The pioneer mothers of that day saw to it that their daughters were brought up to a course of domestic science, right in the home, under their own eye and tutorship.

The following year, in 1838, Miss Beebe went to "Upper Crossing," one mile above the present city of Momence, and there taught school in a room of the William Lacy log cabin, built there in 1833, the first habitation on the Kankakee in eastern Illinois. Here were located the Grahams, the Nichols, the Hills, the Dutchers and others with families of small children sufficiently numerous to make a school of creditable proportions. Miss Beebe lived on the south side of the river and the school house was situated on the north side. She daily ferried herself across the river and back and at the same time took the small children of the south side with her, over and back again at the close of school. At this time, seventy-eight years ago, there still remained a village or two of the Pottawattomi in the near neighborhood of "The Crossing" They mingled on terms of friendly intimacy with the settlers, these children of the forest, who., though, possessed of a keen, childish curiosity, were silent and uncommunicative. Often the orderly decorum of the school room was disturbed for a half-hour at a time when prowling Indian would take it into his head to make them a visit unannounced. Sometimes he would take up his station outside the door. More often he would appear at one of the windows and peer stolidly into the room, his features set and immobile, unflinching and apparently unconcerned although the eyes of teacher and pupil were focused upon him. It was useless to speak, for our primitive friends who thus thought well enough of civilization to call now and the, were deaf to all questioning and dumb to a hopeless degree when it came to giving expression to their thoughts.

Miss Beebe's righteous indignation was early aroused at the manner with which the white man plied the savage appetite with liquor. There was the case of "White Pigeon," a local Pottawattomie chief who was a royal good fellow when sober, but a raging demon when loaded with liquor, despite the pacific quality suggested by the title "White Pigeon.'" She one day sought Joe Barbee, a half-breed, who often served the little pioneer community of Momence and along the river as mediator and minister extraordinary at such times when the Pottawattomi, encamped along the river, imbibed too freely of liquor. He was quite a diplomat and his persuasive arts were often employed, and with good effect, in quieting an Indian surcharged with vile liquor. Miss Beebe remembered that often when "White Pigeon" went on a "High Lonesome," Joe Barbee, of Indian Garden, was sent for post-haste to stay with him until he sobered up. She met up with Joe one day and charged him with this unusual message: "Joe, I want you to tell White Pigeon for me, the very next time you see him, that he is not to drink any more liquor! Now, don't you fail me! Be sure and tell him."

Several days later, when she chanced to meet Joe Barbee again, she asked if he had delivered her message.

"Yes," he answered.

"Well, what did he say," she asked, rather impatiently.

"Well, when I told him he said: 'White man make um, Indian drink um! White man no make um, Indian no drink um!'"

Miss Beebe, school teacher though she was, pondered long and thoughtfully over this message which was the essence of courtesy, directness and brevity. But the more she pondered it the more clearly she realized that White Pigeon, by one brief stroke, had closed the "booze" question as between the two for all time.

In 1839 Lorain Beebe taught school in the Beebetown settlement on the Kankakee. In the year 1840 she went down on the Iroquois river to the settlement known as "Bunkum," in Iroquois county. It was while teaching there that she met

Dr. David Lynds, whom she afterwards married. They made their home on a farm on the south side of the Kankakee near "Upper Crossing," where the Tiffany Brick Works are located today. There were other honors that fell to the lot of Lorain Beebe Lynds other than that of being the first school teacher. When Uncle Sid Vail finally landed a postoffice at his tavern at the settlement a name for the office became a paramount necessity. He named it "Lorain," after his niece. Uncle Sid Vail was a whig in politics and Dr. Lynds was a democrat. Congressman "Long John" Wentworth, of Chicago, was also a democrat who admired Vail personally, but damned his politics. As a matter of good political strategy he deposed Vail as postmaster and gave the job to Dr. Lynds. Lynds moved the office to his place near the "Crossing" and naturally retained the name of "Lorain" as bestowed by Mr. Vail, since the lady had become his wife. Lorain Beebe Lynds was not only the first school teacher, but the first postmistress on the Kankakee in eastern Kankakee county, at that time known as Will. The first official cognomen Momence ever enjoyed was that of "Lorain." With the passing of the postoffice, so passed the name to another field, to supersede for all time the varied titles by which the upper ford had been known for a generation— "Upper Crossing," "Hill's Ford" and "Westport." The place has vanished but the name remains— the name of "Lorain."

From the days of Lorain Beebe's first efforts at teaching school on up to 1850, efforts had been put forth by the settlers to affect some kind of an organization. In the late forties John Strunk, the miller, and William Chatfield were serving as school directors. The early part of the day summer school in 1850 was taught by a Miss Marks, who after-wards became the wife of Dr. Lane. She had some trouble with the pupils before the expiration of the term, and the directors hired Miss C. A. Curtis, sister of Elon and Leroy Curtis, to close the term. Jas. Bennett, who had come to the country that year, was engaged to teach the winter term. There was a squabble over the propriety of scripture reading in the school which came near preventing his appearance as teacher in this school. So, you see, this question was a serious one as far back as seventy-five years ago. The school room was about 16x20, seats were made of puncheon slabs, flat side up, with holes bored in the corners for the wooden legs, and one desk was made of boards wherein were stored the written copies, etc. The pens used in the school were made of goose quills by the master. Among the pupils in attendance at this school were: B. F. Gray, Helen, William and Mary Strunk, James, Martha and Jane Chat- field, Lewis, Fred and Amelia Clark, Harden and Martha Vail, and many others from the families of the VanKirks, Grahams, Edwards, Fenders, Chamberlains, Motts, etc. This school in 1850-1 is said to have had about fifty pupils.

Lorain Beebe Lynds, the pioneer blazer of educational trails in Kankakee county, lived to see the primitive log cabin of one room give way to a stately edifice of stone and brick, the city high school, where hundreds of the city's youth are daily taught by an efficient corps of instructors. She lived to see the development of a land and a people whose chief bulwark is education, on which hundreds of thousands of dollars are spent. When, later on, the city of Momence built another school building, this time on the south side of the river and near the old home of Mrs. Lynds, it was given the name of "The Lorain School," in honor of a well-loved citizen thus distinguished as Kankakee county's first school teacher. She lived to be ninety-three years old, retaining her brightness of mind and keenness of intellect—a frail human link which a breath might dissolve—that for so long bound the yesterday of the "border" with the luxurious era of today.

TWO PIONEER CRONIES

Pierre Brassard, several of whose sons are prominently identified with the business interests of Momence today, and Frank Longpre were hunting partners years and years ago when the great marsh country east of Momence was in its prime. Pierre Brassard died many years ago, but Frank Longpre survived and passed on only recently at the ripe age of ninety. To begin with, there was a racial bond which held them firmly for both were Canadians, and both had the Canadians' inborn instinct for the out of doors, the open trails and the flyways of the feathered hosts of the upper air. Both were at home either in the "blind" or beside the wilderness camp-fire. Each had confidence in the other born of many a campaign together on the upper reaches of the Kankakee or in the Beaver Lake country of eastern Indiana.

In time they became indispensable to one another. No one ever surpassed Pierre Brassard with the shot-gun. He was an artist— a master in the art of shooting. No one ever equaled Frank Longpre in the art of calling geese in the days before the mechanical "squawker" was devised. In this he was a past-master. Frank Longpre's voice, like John McCormick's, was his fortune and, in some respects, showed more cultivation than did that of McCormick. To Pierre Brassard, out on the flyway, it "was the sweetest story ever told," when Frank Longpre was "going good." Working thus together, they made unusual bags of game.

The story is still told of them that one day while returning from the region of Beaver Lake with a load of game they had killed, they noticed, as they drew near the river, numbers of ducks and geese circling over an open- water space which appeared in the river's frozen surface. The air was black with geese and, although they had a load, their hunter's blood thrilled at the prospect. They stationed themselves by the river and Frank Longpre began to "honk." Swiftly the game began to circle to the lure, and as fast as they came within range, Pierre Brassard dropped them. It was little better than slaughter, but such an opportunity was not to be passed by. An hour passed at this point and they had gathered in so many geese that they were nonplused as to what disposition to make of them, for their light wagon was so loaded that not another carcass could be made to stick on. Pierre Brassard finally hit upon a scheme.

"Francois," said he to Mr. Longpre, "wat you say—we hang 'em up on de limb of de tree, and den we come back tomorrow and get dem, hey?" So the geese were hung up in the trees along the river bank according to Pierre's suggestion, hung by their legs high up where the prowlers of the forest could not get at them. And when they had finished the job, they beheld with satisfaction in this out door cold storage the forms of one hundred and thirty-five black Canadian geese! As they resumed their journey towards Momence, presently Pierre Brassard began to chuckle. "Hey, Francois! By Jack! I tell you wot we do wit de boys on de ville; we will mak de grand bet dat we get de mos' geese tomorrow —we bet our jack-knives against theirs—an all we have to do is jes' pick de geese off de roos' on de limb!" And he dug his companion in the ribs with his elbow and the two laughed long and heartily, these two old boys of the wilderness, who thus conspired quietly and "put up a job" on the rest of the hunting fraternity.

PIERRE BRASSARD

This Ancient Tin-Type is the Only Likeness Now Remaining of a well-known Hunter, Trapper and All-Around Frontiersman of Momence. Pierre Brassard Was a Canadian, One of the Finest Shots in the Whole Lake Region. He Was Born to the "Buckskin" of the Frontier and the Life of the Out of Doors. He knew the Kankakee and the Great Marsh Region and was Often Employed as a Guide.

PRANK LONGPRE

He was Brassard's Hunting Partner Whose Specialty was Imitating the "Honk" of a Goose. Old-Timers say of Frank Longpre That he Could Make a Goose Get Down Among the Rushes and Hunt for Him.

AROMA TOWN'S "BEST MAN"

Gus Wiley, who built the first white man's habitation in the timber on the Kankakee at Aroma, and who, some years later, in company with Alvin Wilbur, laid out the townsite of Aroma in 1852, was a character. His people, when he was born, unthinkingly imposed a burden on the name of Wiley by naming him Augustus M. The fates decreed, however, that in the pioneer community in which he lived, he was to be known as "Gus," and also as "Aroma's Best Man." The "Best Man" of the pioneer days was he who was rated as being able to lick his weight in wild-cats, and successfully uphold the dignity and reputation of the community against attack from interlopers from the outside. Wiley was not only a good shot with the old flint-lock rifle, but he was a terror with his fists. He was a consistent and satisfactory performer in the matter of a rough and tumble, such as was the vogue in the days of the border. We digress from the lines of the story long enough to say that the Pacifist is distinctly a twentieth century product. He is the product of our latter- day prosperity—the more or less pampered child of fortune—reared in luxurious ease.

The red blood of pioneer days has been so watered, so diluted and thinned apparently, that the iron of the old days has gone out of it entirely. Such a deterioration of the race made possible the winning slogan of a presidential candidate not so long ago—"He kept us out of war!"

Wiley was a terror and a bear-cat but not of the swashbuckling, insinuating, overbearing type. He had to be stepped on first but, whenever that happened, the response was instantaneous, magnificent. In the days of the old frontier, men stood four-square on their rights, their honor and their reputation, more especially if "that reputation" credited them with being "the best man" in the township. A story illustrating the spirit of the age, is told of grandfather Isaac Legg, who came from Putnam county, Indiana, to Chicago in 1833, and who moved from there to Aroma township sometime in the late thirties. He was on his way to town one day on horseback, while still residing in Putnam county, Indiana, when he chanced to fall in with a stranger. They rode along together and talked of many things, when the stranger chanced to let drop the statement that he was "the best man" in his community. Grandfather Legg lost no time in letting the stranger know that he was the "Best Man" in his bailiwick, and then and there the two slipped from their horses and went at it. Grandfather Legg succeeded in putting it over on his adversary in this instance, after which they remounted their horses and proceeded on their way.

Mr. Martin Van DerKarr relates a story of Gus Wiley in his palmy days. On one occasion, while in Kankakee, Wiley was partaking of an oyster stew in a restaurant, when a Frenchman, from Bourbonnais, somewhat the worse for liquor, walked into the place and inquired, in a loud voice: "Is dat bully from 'Roma, wat dey call Wiley, on dis place?" Wiley was "on dat place," and so informed him, at the) same time asking what he wanted of him. "Sacre, I show you who is de bes' man! I am de bully from Bour-bon-nay, by gar!" Wiley explained briefly but quietly that he was, at that moment, trying to get all the pleasure and satisfaction possible out of his oyster stew; that he would be through in a moment, and if the "Bully from Bour-bon- nay" would not intrude his presence but kindly wait for him on the outside, he would be glad to accommodate him. And then he added significantly: "A bowl of oysters costs twenty-five cents, and I like 'em hot. The pleasure of lickin' you won't cost a damn cent!"

"The Bully from Bour-bon-nay" was not to be put off. He became increasingly boisterous and finally insisted that Wiley did not dare to come outside. Seizing a favorable opportunity, Wiley rose suddenly from the table at which he was sitting, grabbed the bully by the scruff of the neck with his left hand, while his right sought a death-grip on the seat of his trousers. "The Bully from Bour-bon- nay" cut a ludicrous figure thus propelled from the rear by Wiley's giant frame. Straight towards the open door they headed, and, as the Frenchman went through, the velocity of a body falling in space was augmented, at least on the start, by a terrific kick, which landed full and fair. "Now," said Wiley, "you set down and be ca'm. If there's anybuddy you'd like to bid good-by, you'd better do that, too; I'll have them oysters licked up in jist a minute." Wiley returned to the table and resumed the interrupted meal. When he had finished, he paid for it, and then leisurely betook himself to the outside.

In the meantime, the Bully from Bour- bon-nay, whether from the effects of a partial sobering up or a brief interval spent in serious reflection, was not nearly so anxious to annihilate the Bully from 'Roma as he had been. Rather, he desired him as an ally—a friend. He made a proper apology to Wiley for disturbing him while at his meal in the restaurant, acknowledged that, as a bully, he had no business with "the Bully from 'Roma," and, as evidence that the amende honorable on his part was genuine and sincere, invited him to go across the street to a "hard liquor palace" and seal the friendly covenant with a drink.

MR. MARTIN VANDERKARR

Mr. VanDerKarr is a Pioneer of Aroma Township. Hale and Hearty and Active at Ninety. He Left "The Loop" in Chicago in the Early Forties to go Somewhere and Grow Vegetables and be out of the Water. For Years he Raised Cucumbers for the Seed at the Instance of Vaughn, the "Seed Man," of Chicago.

There was a saloon in that day on Court Street where the Fina building now is, and thither they made their way. Not one but many drinks were partaken of during the sojourn of the party there, and under the stimulus of the liquor the Frenchman's drooping courage revived and again became formidable. However, there was this difference in his attitude towards Wiley; instead of wanting to fight him, Wiley had become his especial protege whose reputation was as sacred a thing as his own. He had suddenly switched from antagonist to protector. Turning to the mixed crowd in the saloon, he screamed at the top of his voice: "Hey, you mushrats! Dis ees ma fren, Monsieur Wiley; 'es de Bully from 'Roma! Me? I'm de Bully from Bour-bon-nay! Anyone wat lay one 1-e-e-tle finger on him—sacre battan—'es get hees eyes scratch out, so !" And suiting the action to the word, his face was contorted in an awful grimace, and the extended arms and hooked fingers were truly suggestive of the cruel claws of the wild-cat.

And that was as near as the Bullies of 'Roma and Bour-bon-nay ever came to a mix- up.

Mr. William Spence, a Kankakee resident who knew Wiley well, recalls that on one other occasion Wiley was sought by a neighborhood bully, "a youth to fortune, and to fame unknown," whose only claim to a niche in the hall of fame of that day, was by reason of the sound thrashing Wiley gave him. From Wiley's house, at Aroma, there was a path that led through the thick underbrush to a favorite fishing-hole on the river. Wiley was an enthusiastic fisherman in a day when fishing on the Kankakee was worthwhile, and scarcely a day passed that he did not traverse this wilderness path with his hickory fishing-pole. The unknown bully laid in wait for him one day on this path and, as he appeared, stepped out in front

183

of him and blocked the way. "Are you Gus Wiley?" asked the stranger. "I am," said Wiley; "what can I do for you?"

"I'm going to give you a lickin'," said the stranger seriously.

"All right," flashed Wiley, "off with your coat!'

The stranger pulled his coat. "Why don't you pull yourn," said the stranger, as Wiley threw down his fish-pole and stepped up to him with his coat on. "It's too much trouble fur nothin' " replied Wiley, "git up yer hands and look out fer yourself!" The bout was fast and furious, most too fast and decidedly too furious for the youthful stranger who did not long stand up under the vigorous grueling of this backwoods giant. The fellow was only too glad to acknowledge, finally, that his ideas as regards to licking Wiley had undergone a radical change in the space of five minutes— that he might have been in the right place but the wrong pew. It wasn't Wiley he was looking for after all; it was a fellow who looked a good deal like him! He had done his bit but was conscious of a strong desire "to pass the torch to other hands" before he had fairly got started. And Wiley, after a few sage remarks by which youth might profit, picked up his fishing-pole and went his way to the old fishing-hole on the river.

"GOOD OLD ELDER BURR"

Shakespeare's witty and somewhat caustic observation, "the good is oft interred with the bones," fails utterly in its application to the Rev. S. P. Burr, Momence's first resident minister. After seventy years he is still recalled among the old settlers in and about Momence, and those who are disposed to relate tales concerning him invariably preface their statements with the significant legend, uttered with a notable emphasis and unmistakable unction—"He was a good old man, was Elder Burr!" That he was a good old man, there is no room for reasonable doubt, since saint and sinner, with one accord, after all these years, join heartily in the happy designation at such times when the good old Elder's name is mentioned.

He was the father of Methodism in Momence. By this we do not mean that he was the first to hold religious services in the little river settlement on the Kankakee. There were other circuit riders who preceded him by many years. Enoch Sargeant, a brother of Asher Sargeant, the first settler at Momence, who came to the river in 1835, although not a circuit rider, held preaching services now and then. Elder Morrison, who lived four miles north of the Momence settlement, is a quaint early-day character whose mannerisms and oddities of speech are still recalled. For many years he, with others, traversed the wilderness and brought to the dwellers therein the message of the gospel, besides serving the limited population of that day on the occasion of a wedding, a christening or a funeral. Elder Morrison officiated at the wedding of Daniel Beebe and Nancy Mellen, which was held at the Mellen home situated near the mouth of Exline creek, on December 30,1841. After the ceremony had

185

been duly performed, the Elder, as a fitting finale, offered up a long and fervid prayer, in which, apparently, not one of life's serious problems was left untouched. To the bride's great confusion and embarrassment, the good old Elder petitioned the Almighty to bestow upon this couple a numerous progeny, to be directed always in the way of righteousness.

If the congregations of that day were blunt, practical, "homespun" folk, with little or no education, so, too, were the preachers of the circuit who exhorted them in the language of the old frontier. If, at times, he spoke in rude and homely phrase, if, sometimes, his statements were pointed with the grim, uncouth humor of the pioneer, it was because he was of them and knew them and understood them. Elder Morrison used to say to his congregation: "Brethren, thar will be preachin' here four weeks from this day—wind and weather permittin' ah, and if the green-heads ain't too bad!" It is hard for twentieth century folk to see anything but humor in this statement. It is harder still to realize that "the wind, the weather and the green-heads," were elemental difficulties to be seriously considered at all times by the lowly circuit rider.

Rev. Elisha Springer rode one of the earliest Methodist circuits, established in 1833, extending from Spring Creek, Iroquois county, to Rensselaer, Indiana, and from the Wabash to the Kankakee. He made this circuit in 1842 and preached in some of the outlying districts to the east of Momence. It is recalled that, at times, when he was announcing future services, he would say: "I will hold services here two weeks from today," and then, eyeing the male members of the congregation shrewdly, added the following unusual qualification, "that is, if it ain't a good coon day!"

He knew that if it did happen to be a "good coon day," the male members of the congregation, unable to resist the lure of the coon in the woods, would not be present at the service, however urgent the call of the gospel might be.

The first of the early-day circuits on the Kankakee was that which embraced a circle extending from Joliet to Wilmington, up the river to Momence, thence to Beebe's Grove, Thorn Grove, Crete, Frankfort, etc., over one hundred miles in extent. When in the fall of 1849, the Rev. S. P. Burr was appointed to this circuit, it had been much shortened, so much so that Elder Burr, as he was known by the settlers, found Momence a convenient center from which to make his ministrations. This circuit on which he served was later called the "Beebe Grove Circuit."

As a rule the pioneer settlers were a people of deep and genuine religious convictions. This, however, does not seem to have been the case with the people who constituted the slender population of Momence of that day. The town bore the reputation of being a wide-open, go-as-you-please, free-for-all sort of town and lived up to its reputation. In that day, from 1847 to about 1856, it experienced its greatest prosperity. It then had some five or six stores and something like two hundred inhabitants, to say nothing of the country tributary. The inhabitants of Momence and those who frequented the place were, in the main, typical frontier types. Musk-rat and coon-skin caps and buckskin vests and coats were the rule rather than the exception. If these people were "hard-nosed," (to use the popular vernacular of today), in their attitude towards matters religious, it is not to be taken that they were openly hostile to the circuit rider and his ministrations. They were merely indifferent—decidedly and markedly so—that's all.

Elder Burr was a shrewd, kindly, friendly, practical sort of man who, in addition to these desirable personal qualities, was distinctively a man of parts, as the little community soon came to know. He brought to the little river settlement of Momence the very first buggy that ever came to town. That buggy was a most important asset in one respect at least. It broke down the barrier of cold reserve and indifference on the part of the citizens of Momence as nothing else could. A community might be unmindful of a lowly circuit rider and preacher, and go their way and show little concern in his affairs, so long as he let them alone and did not obtrude too strongly upon the established order of living. But the buggy, of which the Elder made use in making his rounds, proved a decided spur to public interest. In the stores, in the saloons, on the street, wherever men gathered and talked, the buggy, an innovation of surpassing importance to the backwoods settlement of that day, was discussed in all its phases.

Quite unconsciously these people of the old frontier town developed, in time, a substantial respect for this grim old warrior of the cross who possessed not only a buggy, but a fine set of carpenter tools, in the use of which he was very expert. A parsonage was built for the Elder in the fall of 1849. It stood on Locust street just opposite where the ruins of the old brick school house stood for so long. The site later served W. M. Durham as a garden. This parsonage building was 16x24. Chauncey and Albert Chipman, assisted by Rev. Burr himself, were the carpenters who jointly erected this modest domicile. This first parsonage was used up until about the time of the building of the old stone church. At that time W. H. Patterson desired the site to add to his grounds, which later became the Durham home, and arranged with James Mix and the church trustees for an exchange for the present parsonage lot at the corner of Fifth and Range Streets.

John Bennett tells us that in the year 1850 a representative of the Presbyterian faith in the person of Rev. Birze, came to Momence. At that time preaching services were held in the school house, and Elder Burr and Rev. Birze preached on alternate Sabbaths. It happened that on one occasion there was a misunderstanding between the two as to which had the day, both claiming it. Early on that Sunday morning Elder Burr, in order to head off his friend Birze, repaired to the school house, built the fire, swept out and put everything to rights, and then went home to dress for church. When he returned with his wife three-quarters of an hour later, much to his surprise he found friend Birze in full charge. Elder Burr was not slow to grasp the point, and sat down and, for once in his life, listened to a good, old-fashioned Presbyterian sermon.

Elder Burr was returned to this charge by the conference in the year 1851 and thus served the community for two years. An annoying throat trouble, with which he was afflicted, caused him to resign as a regular pastor after 1851, but, for a number of years thereafter, he continued to make Momence his home, preaching occasionally and working at his trade of cabinet maker. For years he had his shop in the Berg building on River street, near the alley. This building is still standing. Elder Burr, in the eyes of the little river settlement, was not only a good man, a good preacher, as preachers went in that day, but a good cabinet maker. He was a most helpful and handy man to have around in a day before the commercial era had superseded the rude arts of pioneer handicraft. Some idea of what this plain, kindly, simple old man meant to the settlement of that day may be gained from the varied services he rendered. He married people; then he made the furniture with which they began housekeeping; when a child was born, he christened it, if the parents so desired ; when a death occurred, he administered spiritual comfort and preached the funeral sermon, besides supplying, by his own handiwork, the queer, angular, six-sided coffin of black walnut in which they were laid away. Truly his was a service many-sided and indispensable. Here and there about Momence may be found in this day examples of the plain.sturdy household furniture that had its origin in the unpretentious shop of the old circuit rider long ago. Time has invested these pieces with memories and given them a value quite out of proportion to the humble materials employed.

Though the Elder was patient and unwearying in the cause of Christianity, aside from a very few families in town and the near countryside, the cause of the gospel did not visibly prosper. Men went their way, but that way led invariably to the saloon and the gambling hells and never to the house of God, except in the case of a funeral. There was one "saving grace" the community had—they would attend a funeral. And, at such times, the Elder, quick to take advantage of an opportunity to snatch a brand from the burning, would exhort his hearers to flee from the wrath to come and take refuge in God's justice.

A notable instance is recalled of a funeral at which the old Elder presided. It was that of the two-year old son of James

190

Nichols, a pioneer and a member of the well-known family of "Uncle Billy" Nichols, who lived three miles northwest of the settlement. The time was about 1855 or 1856. The Nichols were well known and popular among all classes and numbered among their friends almost the entire population of Momence, as well as the settlers of the countryside. The tragic death of James Nichol's little son, John, moved the community to an unusual demonstration of sympathy, evidenced by a remarkable attendance at the funeral.

The little fellow one day in the early summer, was romping through the open doors of the house and out in the yard around the end of the house and back through the open doors in a circuit when, suddenly, from out of doors, the mother heard a piercing scream. Hurrying out she found the child, and the nearby ugly form of a prairie rattle-snake indicated only too plainly to the mother what had happened. On one of the child's ankles appeared two bright red spots where the deadly fangs of the reptile had struck. Such remedies as the pioneer made use of to combat the deadly poison of the rattler were employed, but without avail. The little fellow died within three days. A sorrowful errand for the father was when he sought out Elder Burr, and from his pocket drew forth a string of a certain length whereon appeared a knot a certain distance from one end, indicating roughly the dimensions of a coffin for the toddler, which the Elder then and there proceeded to make.

The funeral was attended by all classes of Momence's mixed population and the Elder therein recognized an opportunity to bring the message of the gospel to a people whom he never met except on the street or on the rare occasion of a funeral. His effort on this occasion was a notable example of vigorous exhortation. For the space of an hour he urged that congregation "to leave off sin and take on righteousness." No sermon of camp-meeting or revival days ever surpassed in earnest intensity this effort of Elder Burr. As one expressed it: "He did everlastingly lambast them on their shortcomings." That audience for days afterwards, felt the moral effect of this appeal of the old parson to their better instincts. His picturization of the evil one, outlined against the fires that glow unceasingly in the abysmal depths of the brimstone pit, was a fearful, awesome thing, the mere recollection of which loomed like the shadow of a spectre standing back of the chair at a feast. Some days later a Momence gambler, a rather likable fellow, on meeting the Elder on the street, asked him point blank why he went after that congregation so hard. The Elder eyed him shrewdly for a moment and replied: "Whenever the devil lets go your coat-tails for a space, that is my opportunity; many of you I never see except at a funeral service! The message of salvation is a vital one whatever the occasion may be!" And the parson smiled a kindly smile so that he to whom his words had been addressed smiled also and remarked: "Elder, you're a trump! In this gospel game you win! You hold aces, kings and queens against ten-spots and deuces!"

From this it will be seen that in the years that followed, there was an increasing respect for the sincere old parson among all classes in the little river settlement of whom, as a matter of truthful acknowledgement, it must be admitted that they were a wild and harum scarum lot. But the leaven of friendliness and kindliness is irresistible and, like "the blood," on which the southerner sets such store, "is bound to tell in time!" A marked deference was shown Elder Burr and men of all types touched the brim of their hat in token of respectful salutation. The riverman, the rounder, the hunter and trapper, who spent much of his time in the wilderness, coming to town now and then that he might fraternize with his fellows, load up with needed supplies and liquor, never passed the parson on the street that he did not remove his pipe with one hand, while with the other he tilted the queer muskrat cap he wore.

The old Elder, amid surroundings forbidding and all but hopeless, nevertheless sowed the seed of friendliness and kindliness with a liberal hand, as if hopeful and confident of the future. Truly, his was a faith fixed firmly and unshakably on the word of God, which says: "Whatsoever a man soweth, that shall he also reap!" And that his faith and his labors were not in vain, behold, after seventy years, wherever recollection goes back to those primitive days, there is this unvarying testimony to his memory—

"He was a good old man, was Elder Burr."

Next to William Lacy and Mr. James Van- Kirk, who settled at the "Upper Crossing" in the fall of 1833, came Robert Hill in the year 1834. He took up a claim on the south side of the Kankakee and immediately constructed a cabin of logs nearby the Chicago-Vincennes trail and opened a tavern. This tavern was destined to become famous for Robert Hill was of the broad, genial, expansive Southern type, a bon-vivant whose stories and cheer and hospitality soon became the "talk of the trail." These qualities, indispensable to a successful tavern keeper, were further aided, sustained and abetted by "Ma" Hill, than whom, no better cook ever basted a turkey or dipped her hands in flour anywhere on the trail between Vincennes and Chicago.

In that early day of the border there were taverns that had achieved something of a reputation with the traveling public of that day, notably the "Buckhorn Tavern," situated south of the Kankakee in the forks of the trail in the near outskirts of the present town of Donovan, Iroquois county. A former townsman, the late Major R. J. Hanna, years ago gave us an idea of the menu of this old-time hostelry in 1857. He was a member of the surveying party that laid out the line of the T. P. & W. Railway. They were in the immediate neighborhood of where the town of Sheldon stands today, and there was but one lone shack visible in all the country roundabout. The man of the shack was too poor to have a floor in it. He was so poor that he could provide nothing more than potatoes with the jackets on and a dish of sow-belly, at which the stomachs of the men revolted. They paid for the dinner they did not touch and then, to quote Mr. Hanna's words: "We sent our Irishman five miles to the old Bunkum Buckhorn

Tavern to order supper for five hungry men. We arrived there
shortly after dark and Oh, my countrymen, what a banquet
was there provided! There was a puncheon floor, a puncheon
table, and puncheon boards for seats, but all clean as wax. In
the center of the table was a large dish filled with mashed
potatoes as white as snow, with a tablespoonful of golden
butter in the center; cream, snowy biscuits, and a roast joint
of beef that would have done honor to King Arthur's Round
Table. We sat down to this feast with stomachs twelve hours
distant from breakfast."

Robert Hill within the short space of a year or so, found his
log hostelry altogether inadequate to the demands of the
wilderness public. Such was his fame, so completely did he
dominate the spot that the hosts of freighters frequenting the
"Chicago-Vincennes Road" called this crossing of the
Kankakee "Hill's Crossing." There was everything to indicate
that here, where the travel converged, was a most likely spot
for a town and Hill, imbued with this idea, proceeded to build
a two-story frame structure that would have been a credit to
any town of that day. The building of this house took place
about 1840. The framework was hand-hewn, the sheathing
and smaller timbers being furnished by the saw-mill at
Momence, a mile away. The finishing lumber was hauled
from Chicago. With the building of the new structure, the
reputation of "Hill's Tavern" grew apace and, for a space of
ten years or more, enjoyed a remarkable run of patronage.
Men on the road would put themselves to much trouble and
inconvenience in order that they might put up for the night at
"Hill's Tavern." There they were sure of a congenial company
and the best of fare.

What an interesting insight into the life of that day might have been gathered from the conversation and stories of the pioneers themselves as they drew round the hospitable hearth in the bar-room of this wayside inn? What stories of hardships, adventure and romance that filled the lives of the pioneers, were bandied about when the Hoosier from the Wabash, the Yankee from the east, the riverman and the hunter of the woods and prairies thus met? The historian of today would have found in the varied types that patronized the "Hill Tavern" of 1840, abundant material for a volume, replete with historical fact and the humor of the frontier. It is even hinted that Landlord Hill himself could have supplied the substantial elements of a volume, single-handed and alone, that is, when he was feeling his best.

There is one story told of Hill which was so highly esteemed by the border populace that it has, fortunately, outlived the years. This tale bears the modest title "How Hill Made Change." Hill was a convivial fellow and, in his later years, enjoyed the flowing bowl as well as the companionship of his old-time friends. On one occasion he had for his guests, James Dickey, father of the Dickey family, William Nichols, (Uncle Billy, the father of most all of the Nichols), and John Hayhurst, father of the Hayhursts. It was a particularly joyful time, for most all of them had come to the country at the same time, in 1834, '35 and '36, and they were doubtless deep in the reminiscences of the old days. Hill was pretty well organized—well lighted up—as they say of one who shows a proper appreciation of the social amenities, when he was suddenly interrupted by a stranger who demanded attention in a decidedly preemptory tone.

Hill was in no hurry to leave off in the middle of a good story and, accordingly, paid no attention to the fellow. The stranger, not to be put off in this manner, became boisterous and commanded attention of Hill who, much to everybody's surprise, gave it to him in the shape of a thrashing, then and there. Naturally, the stranger was indignant, and requested to know where he could find a justice-of-the-peace. Hill told him there was no use going to all that trouble. He could get justice right there. Here was a jury of three good men who had witnessed the assault, and they could retire and make up a verdict, and thus dispense with all red-tape. The man consented to this novel proposition, and Dickey, Nichols and Hayhurst retired and discussed the affair. They decided that Hill had struck the man four times and, as a penalty, they declared that he should pay the man a dollar for each blow and give him his dinner free of cost. The verdict thus rendered by Hill's friends was accepted as satisfactory by both sides, and Hill ordered the dinner prepared. After the man had finished his repast Hill handed him a five-dollar bill. Hill had fifty cents coming to him. The stranger could not make the change and so announced. "All right," said Hill, "I make the change," and, forthwith, he landed the fifth blow between the eyes that landed the stranger well up in the corner of the bar-room. The jury helped the fellow to his feet and as they did so, they advised him that although the difference in change now laid in his favor, he had best run along about his business and let Hill keep it.

The register of the Hill Tavern, if they had such a thing, and if it were accessible in this day, would show the names of individuals afterwards famous in the business and political world. Congressman "Long John" Wentworth, of Chicago, used to stop here during his campaigns. At an Old Settlers' meeting, held in the year 1880, at Old Bunkum, now Iroquois, in Iroquois county, "Long John" Wentworth was one of the speakers and related an interesting personal experience at the "Hill Tavern." In the year 1843, he was running for Congress, and his district embraced about one-fourth of the state, comprising the east half from Vermilion county north. On one occasion he delivered a speech at some town west of Chicago, and the next day but one was to deliver a speech at Bunkum. It was a long drive and he started the night before, after delivering his first speech. A little after noon the next day he arrived at "Hill's Tavern" and procured his dinner. He then explained to Landlord Hill that he had been riding all the previous night and asked if he could not lay down for a three-hour nap. He was shown into a room adjoining the dining room, where he threw himself across the bed and sought sleep. Presently he heard the voices of two young ladies, whom he supposed to be Hill's daughters, in the adjoining room.

"I believe that is Wentworth, the man who is running for Congress," he heard a voice say.

"No, it can't be," said the other, "for Wentworth is nearly seven feet tall, and that man isn't that big."

"Well," said the other, "I noticed he was awful big, and I'll bet it's him."

There was considerable discussion as to the identity of the sleeper when one of the girls suggested that they measure him and thus make sure. There was considerable giggling and bantering back and forth, but finally stealthy steps were heard approaching the bedroom door. "Long John" stretched himself at full length and started to snore in a way that fairly jarred the roof. Inch by inch the door opened noiselessly and a pair of mischievous eyes peeped from behind the edge of it. A warning finger was laid on her lips as a sign of caution to the other, and then she whispered: "He's sound asleep!" They then procured a string, tip-toed into the room and forthwith measured him from the crown of his head to the extreme tip of his big toe. The girls were highly elated at their achievement and the result of the measurement appeared to settle conclusively the fact that it was "Long John" Wentworth himself and no one else.

With the passing of the pioneers who first settled in the near environs of "Hill's Tavern," on the Kankakee, there passed into oblivion also memories of the numerous dances and social functions held there from time to time from 1835 up to 1850. Another entertaining volume might be written of these affairs if the past could but speak. "Hill's Tavern" was a spot of happy memories for the belles and beaux and settlers of the nearby wilderness who were wont to gather there. Mr. and Mrs. Hill, who made the Tavern famous, were even more famous as entertainers. There was a wholesome heartiness to the welcome they ex-tended to these friends, and the more of noise and bustle and confusion, the topsy-turvier things became about the house the better Pa and Ma Hill liked it. There was always a good time at Hill's, and that statement goes as it lays.

About the last that is remembered of the tavern was a grand ball, given by Hill in the spring of 1850, during the days of the California gold excitement, in honor of a number of residents who were leaving the following day under the captaincy of Philip Worcester, for the gold fields of the new Eldorado. Among them was Hill's son, Sam, a well-known character in that day. There was a most notable attendance at this function and the fun was fast and furious and lasted until the break of day. Several hours later Captain Worcester and his men on horseback and with wagons carrying supplies, set forth bravely on the trail that extended more than half-way across the continent. They set out on the river trail on the west bank of the Kankakee and Luther Gleason, a lad of nine years, watched the cavalcade as it passed their home on the river, (now the Alice Payne farm), and saw them turn into the old trail that branched from the river road at the point where the old Rice cemetery is, and lost itself in the unbroken prairie to the west. Captain Worcester, stiff and military looking on his charger, led the van. There was a man carrying the stars and stripes, and following were men on horseback and in the wagons. Among those who made up the party that left Momence were: Albert and Horace Worcester, John Treverbaugh, Sam Hill, Jake Nichols, A. C. Beadle, John Beebe, Elias VanDeKarr and Henry Case. There were others of the party from the neighborhood of Momence, but their names are not obtainable in this day.

Through the medium of a diary now in the possession of John H. Nichols, kept by his uncle, John E. Hill while on the memorable overland trip to California, the following particulars are obtained. The party left Momence on the 11th of March, 1850. Those of the party mentioned in the diary are: John E. Hill, S. M. Hill, John Yates, Washington Allen, P. Thatcher, I. Rutter, William Nichols, T. B. Snapp and J. R. Haddon. Each of these men rode a horse and led a pack-animal. They went to Bourbonnais, Wilmington, Galesburg, and then to Memphis, Tennessee, and from there to St. Joe, Missouri, where they outfitted, leaving there on May 13th, 1850. John E. Hill and party left California for home on board a ship called "The Olive Branch," but he died en route and was buried at sea in January, 1851.

At Bourbonnais the ranks of the gold seekers were reinforced by a goodly number, and upon reaching Wilmington three or four more were added, so that there was probably a company of thirty or forty men who started out under the guidance of Captain Philip Worcester. In that day of the fifties, the Hill Tavern had lost much of its patronage, for the bridge across the Kankakee at that place had been carried out in 1849 and Momence, one mile to the west, had forged to the front so that the freighters found the place more to their liking and stopped there on their trips to and from Chicago. One by one the business people of Hill's Crossing dropped down the river to Momence and, in the course of time, the Hill Tavern was moved, building and all. The building was owned for many years by John Lundstrum and occupied the site at the corner of River and Market streets. The building was torn down only a few years ago, and thus passed out of existence one of the most notable landmarks in eastern Illinois.

AN IMPROMPTU DOUBLE WEDDING

It is, perhaps, too much to expect, that a story with a title so tame as the foregoing, will cause even a ripple of interest in the public mind of today. The keynote of the Twentieth Century is "Progress," and nowhere in our social and economic structure is the peculiar progress of the age better illustrated than in the ceaseless grind of our divorce courts, and the columns of the daily press wherein are set forth in nauseating detail, the conjugal infelicities of the times in which we live. It would seem that "speed" is a more becoming term than "progress." Of course, there are and always have been, all sorts of curious people in the world, accustomed to doing all kinds of peculiar stunts and it may be that twentieth century folk, who have progressed to a point where, from sheer ennui, they knock one an-other in the head, or seek a divorce, or simply pull up stakes and vamoose as the easiest way out of a bad situation, may, after all, get a thrill out of this tale of old frontier days.

In our search for the unusual in the way of happenings of frontier days, there was the incident of the two fellows who got together and traded wives, and the other incident of the impromptu double wedding that bobbed up continually whenever an old-time resident became reminiscent and invited one back of the veil to glimpse those treasures which the memory holds worthwhile. He would tell you that over in east of Momence, in the sand and scrub contiguous to the Indiana state-line, there lived in the early days two men and their wives. One of them proposed one day that they trade wives. The other was only mildly interested. He thought he deserved something to boot on the trade. They were both poor as church mice, hence the question of "boot" was a poser. The man who had proposed the trade finally bethought him of a load of hickory poles which he had laboriously hewn out of the timber, and these he tendered with the proviso that the recipient was to come and get them. The offer was accepted and the exchange made, and these meager facts as hereby set forth, are solemnly affirmed by many and many a one of our most reliable citizens. With regard to the impromptu double wedding, many with whom we talked had heard of it, yet none were able to recall the names of the principals nor any of the incidents attending this unusual affair of the frontier. We came at last to look upon it as a pet tradition of the old-time populace, something to regard indulgently and pass by with a smile, until one day, Mrs. America Brosseau asked if we had ever heard of it, and then proceeded to give some of the details.

To begin with Mrs. Brosseau stoutly avers that the story of which we thought so lightly is absolutely true. The couples involved were residents of Bourbonnais township, as we know it today, and, presumably, lived in the near vicinity of the Samuel Davis home on Davis Creek and the Bourbonnais Road. The time was of the late thirties. Mrs. Brosseau recalls that the Davis home was a general rendezvous for the French-Canadian residents of Petite Canada, the prairie settler and the neighborhood "squatter." Davis, in addition to supplying the more urgent needs of the frontier household in the way of sugar, tea and coffee, had always on hand a generous supply of whiskey which he dispensed in quantiles or by the glass as desired. Hence, we may know that there was something of conviviality added to these nightly gatherings at the Davis home, after a drink or two had served to mellow the spirit and unloose the tongue. And if the men found pleasure and interest in these oft-repeated tales, so, too, the old dames who gathered in the ample ingle-nook of the old- fashioned fire-place of the Davis home with cob-pipes that steamed blue like the witching fumes of an incense-pot, found an appetizing flavor in ancient gossip—a new thrill in the more than "twice-told tales." As a child, Mrs. Brosseau says, she has listened to these tales, wide-eyed and serious, holding fast to the maternal skirts meanwhile.

Mrs. Brosseau's memory has fortunately preserved to us the names of the men concerned in this unique affair, Dorion Tetreault and Pete Volkenburg, the one a sort of coureur de bois, or rover, and the other of much the same stripe as Tetreault, was regarded in the parlance of the frontier as a "squatter." By some strange lapse of memory she cannot recall the names of the women, except that one of them was known as Josette and the other Mary. It was at a gathering at a neighboring cabin where these young people, among others, were present, that it was proposed to hold a mock wedding. The young men were more than willing candidates for the event, and tradition even winks mysteriously and intimates as much for the young women. They paired off and solemnly took the marital vows and later "jumped the broom-stick," after which he who had conducted this unusual service (who claimed to have been a justice-of-the- peace at one time in his life), read a chapter from the Bible in a voice decidedly shaky, halting and uncertain, and then pronounced them "man and wife."

Congratulations were showered upon the newly wedded pairs, and all sorts of good natured raillery, such as an occasion of this kind sanctions among friends, was indulged in. Others of the company busied themselves setting back the scanty furniture and clearing the floor. A backwoods fiddler, with his battered violin, appeared conveniently from somewhere, and, seated upon an improvised throne in a corner of the room, the raucous strains of the fiddle, as he tuned the instrument, warned the company that everything was in readiness for a regular, old-fashioned "hoe-down" or "shindig." That mark of distinguished consideration which the frontier residents of that day sought to bestow upon the "newly-weds," found expression chiefly in this outburst of good will, with its laughter, good natured chaffing and music. For hours this happy, care-free people of the old frontier danced to the tune of "the Bumble Bee," which was a favorite, varied now and then by a cotillion, the figures of which were called by one of their number, a more or less disheveled figure who, between calls, pulled steadily on a big, black pipe, and, by way of variation, spat heavily now and then into the nearby fire-place.

There were intervals in the dance of which the men took advantage to get "a nip of liquor," while the "ladies," to appease appetites made voracious by the unusual exercise, partook of "light refreshments," or, in the parlance of the frontier, "a snack." This "snack" consisted of whatever might be procured by scraping the cupboard to the bare boards. Therefore, those who helped themselves, seized upon that which appealed most to the taste—a doughnut, a piece of maple sugar or a biscuit, spread with the dark, rich red of the wild plum. One buxom lass with an appraising eye, succumbed to the lure of a cold corn pone which she spread liberally with flakes of ham-fat and bacon "drippings," and then devoured with numerous outward signs of satisfaction, afterwards wiping the tips of her fingers and her lips on the hem of her "linsey-woolsey." The "caller" must have gotten an inspiration out of this sight of the buxom lass and the corn pone, for, in the cotillion that followed, his genius framed the following, which was a take-off, apparently—

"Meet your partner—

Hit 'er on the head,

If she don't like biscuits Give 'er corn bread;

Keep a hookin' on—

Upon the breaking up of the dance Mr. and Mrs. Tetreault and Mr. and Mrs. Volken- burg were overwhelmed anew by their friends, who wished them all sorts of good luck in their matrimonial venture, although it had, on the whole, been somewhat unpremeditated. But why let a little thing like that interfere? Surely they would some time marry! The wedding had been duly solemnized; the vows had been made before witnesses; the event had been gloriously celebrated by the neighbors of the countryside! What more could anybody ask? And then as if to clinch the arguments already set forth and remove any element of doubt that may have lingered in the minds of the contracting parties themselves, he who had once been a justice-of-the-peace announced ponderously, "You-all is jes' as much married as though you had paid me five dollars apiece." Such an enlightening and convincing statement from the lips of so august a personage was, apparently, all-sufficient. The principals in the affair were all more or less willing to accept the situation, only—it was so sudden, you know—and the "ladies" so flustered for the time being that, if they hesitated for the moment, it was not to be regarded as a sign of disapproval altogether. And in this manner, so old-time gossip affirms, were the ranks of the Benedicts augmented in the little settlement that had its beginning near unto that of "Petite Canada."

There was much of spirited conversation, much of jollity and laughter as the crowd set forth on the dimly lighted trails that led in a round about way through the woods to their homes, and where a trail diverged, there, for a moment, the party would linger that congratulations might be renewed and friendly admonitions repeated. An owl high up in the dead top of a jack-oak and dimly outlined against the waning moon, whose nocturnal reveries had thus been rudely shattered, emitted a terrific "T'whoo! T'wh-o-o! and the still watches of the night were made fairly clamorous by the oft-repeated echo of "Who! Wh-o-o! Wh- o-o-o!" "Ah," said a voice—it was that of the buxom lass of the corn pone—"The man in the moon wants to know who we are! Well, then, if you are so anxious and must know, it is Mr. and Mrs. Tetreault and Mr. and Mrs. Volken- burg on their wedding trip home!" And the outburst that followed this sally of frontier wit so upset and discomfited Br'er Owl that he spread his wings in ignominious flight.

Concerning most marriages of an unusual nature, such as the foregoing, the chronicler thereof is privileged to say "that they lived happily ever after," and, in this particular instance, the reader is justified in accepting the statement without question. More than that, popular gossip of that early day ascribes to these wedded couples a devotion and constancy above reproach, as well as a fair measure of prosperity as prosperity was reckoned in the old days of the border. The gossips of that day even went so far as to preserve to posterity the interesting details of a conversation, said to have taken place between the heads of the respective houses of Tetreault and Volkenburg when, after ten days of wedded bliss, they had settled back into the old, accustomed, shiftless habits of wilderness life. They met one day, Dorion and Pete, as they had often met, down on the river by the old Yost saw-mill, where the fishing was especially good.

Says Pete: "Say, Dorion, how are you and Josette getting along, anyway?"

"Ah," says Dorion in reply, "Josette and me, we git 'long lak two HP kitten—jes' lak two tortle dove! She split de wood, she mak de fire, she fetch de water, she mak de breakfas' an de dinner and de supper; an w'en I light de pipe, she say, 'now, Dorion, don' you move. I fetch you one coal from de fire!' Ah, Pierre, Josette is jes' de one for me! I tell youse, Pierre, I wouldn't tak a honered dollar for Josette if I couldn't git 'noder jes' so good!" And thus lulled by the memory of Josette's many virtues, warmed by the sun's genial rays, at peace with himself and all the world, there rose to his lips unconsciously, so it seemed, an ancient chanson of the voyageur that had lingered for generations in the blood—

> "Each returning springtime
> Brings so much that's new,
> All the fickle lovers
> Changing sweethearts too.
> The good wine soothes and gives me rest,
> While love inspires and fills my1 breast.
> All the fickle lovers Changing sweethearts still,
> I'll keep mine forever,
> Those may change who will!"

THE RIVER NAVIGATION PROJECT

The coming of the Illinois Central railroad to Kankakee in 1853 was most inopportune for the success of an ambitious development enterprise launched as far back as 1846, when the Illinois legislature passed a special act incorporating the Kankakee & Iroquois Navigation and Machinery Company. This company was organized with a capital stock of $100,000, divided into shares of $50 each. The purposes of the company, as set forth in a pamphlet issued in 1847 were, briefly, "the improvement and navigation of the Kankakee and Iroquois rivers, the creation of water power on said streams and the building and erecting of mills and machinery of all kinds on or near said streams. The said company shall have the power to improve as aforesaid, the navigation of said streams, from the point on the said Kankakee river which is intersected by the Kankakee feeder for the Illinois & Michigan Canal, up the said river to the Indiana State line; and from the mouth of the Iroquois, near Waldron, up to the same Indiana State line."

These rivers traversed a considerable territory of exceedingly rich country which, upon its settlement and development, was sure to furnish a tremendous volume of business which would be handled exclusively by the new company. The project had much to commend it as a sound business venture and the stock of the company was readily disposed of among business men and settlers along the streams. The plans of the company further provided for eight dams, the first one below Wilmington and the last one at Momence. The dam at Momence was to cost $2,755 and was to have been provided with a six-foot lift costing $4,500 more. The only expense counted on above Momence was $500 for a "draw" in the bridge at "Upper Crossing," or Westport. The Company's prospectus of that day further states that 30,000 bushels of wheat grown south of the river were annually hauled over the bridge at "Upper Crossing," or Westport, in that early day. Nearly all of the promoters of this ambitious project were Wilmington men. Dr. Hiram Todd, of Rockville, owner of many thousands of acres of valuable river lands on the Kankakee and Iroquois, was interested in the scheme. Wonderful developments were predicted in the region of Rock Creek, Waldron, Momence, on the Kankakee, and for Sugar Island, Plato and Middleport, on the Iroquois.

During the years of the late forties and the early fifties, when the affairs of the Navigation Company loomed encouragingly, people were attracted to Waldron. Its location in the heart of this vast agricultural territory and at the junction of the rivers made it the logical site for a town of real consequence commercially. The Wilburs, of Momence, interested themselves in a milling enterprise and also established a store. Seth Wells, prominently identified with the growth and development of Momence, built a three-story hotel of wood on the corner across the street north from Hoke's store, in Waldron, in 1851. Luther Gleason says that this hotel had the best dancing floor to be found anywhere in the county. The building was later destroyed by fire. The old barn which still stands on the back of the lots occupied by Wells' hotel, had its timbers hewn and framed and was first erected at Momence. Some say that Wells took it down and moved it to Waldron and re-erected it where it stands today. Others think this was done by the Wilburs. Wells had a penchant for three-story buildings. After building the one at Waldron, he later, in 1856, built a three-story brick on the present site of 4he

Central House in Momence. It is said that while the walls were being laid, Wells had a quart bottle of whiskey cached therein. But the bottle did not remain there overnight. Some scalawag pulled down the freshly laid wall and appropriated the booze unmindful of the fact that whiskey was so cheap as to make the effort hardly worthwhile. Wells was the moving spirit in the erection of the Worcester & Lane hall at River and Range streets. He had the foundations up and the materials all on the ground for this three-story building, when he suddenly made up his mind to go to California. He sold to Hannibal Worcester and Dr. J. C. Lane, who finished the present building.

To return to the affairs of the Navigation Company—considerable money had been spent and the improvements as scheduled had actually been extended as far as "Polly's Riffles," a few miles this side of Wilmington, when the bubble burst, due to the building of the Illinois Central Railroad. The hour had struck wherein was ushered in that great era of progress and development which is the most amazing thing in our civilization. After all, the story of progress is largely the story of

"Transportation." The river was the pioneer's natural ally in the days of the "Covered Wagon" and the ox-team. It furnished cheap transportation besides power to grind his wheat and corn and saw the lumber for his wilderness abode. Our friends at Momence, who had depended upon the Navigation Company, while acknowledging the superiority of the newly-built railroad, never-the-less continued to make use of the river for a considerable time. After the coming of the railroad and the locating of Kankakee City, John Paradis, of Momence, constructed the first steamboat to operate on the

Kankakee. This was in 1854. This boat could proceed no farther than Waldron on account of the dam.

Mr. S. W. Skelly, who, as a youth, was first a resident of Kankakee and later of Waldron, or Aroma Park, recalls that shortly after the building of the railroad, in 1853, power boats were placed on the Kankakee for the purpose of conveying freight and passengers to and from Waldron and Kankakee and also between Momence and Kankakee. There were two boats. The one operated by John Paradis was a steamboat, according to Mr. Skelly. The steamboat plied between Momence and Waldron but, on account of the dam, could not proceed farther downstream. The Momence boat steamed into the mill-race at Waldron and there discharged and took on its cargo. The boat operated between Waldron and Kankakee was a flat-bottomed affair with a large stern-wheel. The power was supplied by two horses walking on an inclined endless apron, or tread-mill. This boat was owned by E. R. Beardsley, a man prominently identified with the early activities of the village. A man by the name of Fuller furnished the horses that operated the tread-mill. Quantities of merchandise were thus handled and interchanged by these primitive boats plying between Momence and Waldron and the railroad at Kankakee. There were days when the mill-race levee at Waldron held large cargoes of sacked wheat, barrels of flour, bundles of hides, casks of wine and barrels of whiskey from the distillery at Momence, awaiting transport to the railroad at Kankakee. And on the return up-river, these boats were laden with merchandise brought by the railroad to Kankakee, consigned to points up-river. These boats made one round trip a day. In the meantime, the Beardsley boat at

Waldron, was used as a ferryboat, and was thus reasonably busy from sun-up until dark.

Later in the fifties, Ezra Wetmore, who owned and carried on the present Wetmore farm on the Kankakee between East Court street and Momence, put on the river a forty- foot flatboat which plied between Momence and Waldron, more particularly during the season when the prairie roads were made impassable for heavy loads by the rains. This barge of Wetmore's drew two feet of water, and was drawn by a horse attached to a long line. Sometimes, when the wind was favorable, a large sail would be hoisted and the horse, for the time, was dispensed with. Hugh Wetmore says that as a youth, he has made many and many a trip to Waldron and back astride the horse. This boat carried large cargoes of wheat and corn to Waldron and from there it was hauled to Kankakee by teams. Returning from Waldron, the boat's cargo was more often lumber. On one trip down the river Mr. Wetmore says the boat became lodged on a boulder in the river in the near vicinity of Saddler's Island. They worked nearly all night shifting the cargo to the other end of the boat, and finally succeeded in releasing it. The rates for this service were decidedly modest as compared with the rates of today.

J. B. Wicks operated a daily stage line from Momence to Kankakee in that early day and carried the mail for a number of years. With the building of the C. D. & V. railroad to Momence in 1869, Momence ceased to depend on Kankakee as formerly. But, in this luxurious era of the Twentieth Century, the entente cordiale has been resumed, apparently, to the great advantage of both cities. These places are now united by a magnificent concrete roadway and luxurious coaches that rival the comfort and speed of the railways are at your service every two hours during the day. The temptation is too great! We just can't stay away! The "Dixie Highway" has robbed Momence's Main Street of its very name! It means more to them than the best railway they have! The world now strolls through the open doors of Momence and Kankakee, in high-powered cars that out-rival express and limited trains. The world is on wheels! The man from Maine, and Manitoba, and New York, and New Orleans, and Los Angeles and San Francisco whisk by each other and say hello and goodbye, and wave a friendly salute! We have seen in this sketch how the dawn of the railroad era dissipated the dreams of the Navigation Company of the Kankakee and the Iroquois rivers. After seventy years the hour has struck when railway men in high places are jumpy, and nervous and distracted over the problem that confronts them. For the world is on wheels, and the freight is mostly on trucks! One fifth and better, of Illinois five or six millions own and operate machines, and other sweating millions who haven't them, hope to have them soon! And the railways hope to solve the problem by raising the rates! This is a generation born to the fabled "silver spoon in the mouth," and but a single sou in the wallet, in many cases. The world is on wheels today—"some in rags, some in tags, and some in velvet gowns!" But they all thrill at this touch of luxury which "makes the whole world kin."

THE CATHEDRAL OF THE PRAIRIE

*The Cottonwood with a Story, Which Stands in the Dooryard of the
Alice Payne Farm, on the Banks of the Kankakee.*

THE CATHEDRAL OF THE PRAIRIE

Let us say at the outset that this is a story, a true story, of a cottonwood tree—we were going to say, a humble cottonwood—but that would be a misnomer. The word humble ill becomes the rugged, stately magnificence of this particular tree, said to be the largest in the county, which graces the residential door- yard of the Alice Payne farm, midway between East Court street bridge and the village of Aroma Park, on the west bank of the Kankakee. "The Woods were God's First Temples," but this particular cottonwood, "majestic, isolated, grand," is a cathedral among temples that dot the countryside in this fair valley of the Kankakee. There is no other term quite so fitting—that expresses so much and so truthfully.

Cathedrals and temples are not built in a day, as we know. It is a long, tedious, laborious, heart-wearing process wherein the first effort shows little, and suggests little of the glory to follow. Generations of men worked below ground on the foundations of stately St. Peter's, of Rome and were followed by still other generations who spent their lives and faded into the twilight of the ages without glimpsing the transcendent genius of Raphael and Michelangelo, to whom, apparently, omnipotence gave the triple powers of architect, sculptor, painter. So, in a way, with our "Cathedral of the Prairie." From the days of its nascent life when, as a feathery atom instinct with the germ of life, borne by the winds of chance, it fell, unnoticed of men, on the prairie land of Eber Gleason and was nurtured by rain and sun and the rich prairie soil, and sprouted and grew, and sent forth a tiny root downward,

216

which was the foundation, and a tender shoot upward which the passing years have erected finally into a superstructure of impressive dimensions and perfected symmetry.

On the incompleted life cycle of this cottonwood eighty years are registered and vouched for within the memory of the pioneers. An amazing and interesting feature of this cottonwood was that it was lucky, even as some men are said to be lucky. Just around the corner lurked a kindly fate ready to intervene when the great hour struck, so that men who knew of the incident were moved to say that the cottonwood was lucky as to the particular situation in which it germinated and grew; that it was lucky in the possession of an unusual vitality; above all, that it was lucky in having for a friend, when it most needed a friend, a merciful man, a kindly man —one with the soul and the vision of a poet.

In 1838, when Eber Gleason took up this piece of land on the west bank of the Kankakee, after having driven all the way overland from distant Vermont, he built his log cabin in an open space, devoid of tree or shrub, very near to the present highway. Here Eber Gleason died as early as 1847. He left a widow and a family of small children. Luther Gleason, who was born on the place in 1841, says that he still marvels at how the mother ever reared that family with so very little to go on. Truly that providence which was mindful of a tree, lent a helping hand to the mother in her hour of need.

The sixty acres comprising the Gleason farm of that day, after the death of Eber Gleason were rented to Ralph Parsons, then a youth. Twenty acres of the sixty were still raw prairie and, on that day when Parsons with his black ox team hitched to a breaker started in to turn over the sod, there opened an epoch filled with startling experiences for the trim, slender, two-year old cottonwood whose trunk, about the size of one's index finger and which had attained a height of three or four feet, waved cheerily above the grass and prairie flowers in the far-flung sunshine. As the plowing progressed and furrow on furrow of rich, fat, sleek prairie soil appeared, the doom of the cottonwood became more pronounced. Nearer and nearer the furrows crept until at last, the cattle as they passed, tempted by the rich green leaves, mouthed them and tore them viciously, and the plow, as it passed, toppled the dainty little cottonwood to one side, and Ralph Parsons, as he followed in the furrow, moved by an idle whim, leaned over and picked it up. How prosaic! How common-place!

At the end of the field Parsons stopped the cattle for a moment "to let them blow," and busied himself meanwhile brushing away the "greenheads" that they might rest free from the attacks of these murderous pests, for he was a humane and merciful man, was Parsons. For the remainder of the afternoon he carried the cottonwood switch and, whenever a stop was made, employed it vigorously in brushing the flies. When he left the field that night he brought the switch with him and threw it down in the barnyard. Here the Gleason boys, Audery and Luther, found it and had great fun chasing each other with it. Later, they straddled it and rode it about the yard and youthful imagination invested the cottonwood switch with all the realty of a prancing steed.

That night the cottonwood laid out under the stars in the backyard of the Gleason home, just where the boys dropped it root trunk, branch and all above ground, a thing forlorn, abandoned, yet holding tenaciously to a spark of life.

The following morning, by what fortunate chance, by whose suggestion is not now recalled, the diminutive cottonwood, a wreck of its former self, ragged and bedraggled, shorn of the trim grace and beauty of twenty-four hours ago, was planted in the yard just where it stands today. Ralph Parsons dug the hole and sifted the soil lightly above the roots, while the boys, moved to unusual activity by Parsons's glowing optimism, which pictured this runt of a tree as a great, great big one someday, fairly wore themselves out hauling water with which they deluged it that first day it came to live in Gleason's backyard. It was an interested and loving service that Parsons and the boys extended in their efforts to save the tree, but, for a space, it seemed like labor expended in vain. The cottonwood hesitated and drooped and the larger leaves gradually assumed a jaundiced appearance, whereat Ralph Parsons would feel of them, much as a physician feels of a patient's pulse, and shake his head gravely when, by the mere touch, the leaf detached from the limb. Some weeks later it was decided that an operation was necessary, so four of the primary branches were cut off. Little by little the tree perked up and rounded to, and by fall gave evidence that the life-current had been re-established, and among the youngsters of the Gleason household there was great joy in consequence.

The following year and the next, and the next year after that, this cottonwood waif did marvelously well, and assumed the proportions of a tree whose top was especially shapely and symmetrical. Where it stood in the backyard there was now a generous splash of shade where formerly the afternoon sun burned fiercely. And here, for a brief noonday siesta, Ralph Parsons would often betake himself and sit in quiet contemplation of its rugged strength and beauty and dream betimes of the strange part fate played in the life of a man and a cottonwood tree. If a stranger happened to be present then Ralph Parsons would relate the story of the tree, omitting not the slightest detail of its infantile biography, dwelling particularly on how it once served as a fly-brush, how the boys rode it about the yard, how it laid uncared for all night in the yard, and how nearly it came to giving up the ghost once it was planted. Ralph Parsons loved that tree with a deep and genuine affection that grew with the years, expanding as the tree expanded and mounted higher and higher.

Ten years, and the cottonwood was a lusty thing, bursting with life, instinct with youth and grace and beauty. Twenty years, and it looked down from still greater heights, and gave promise even then that it was the progeny of giants. Thirty years, and from far off on the road, Ralph Parsons on his way to visit it, as he often did, beheld great, branching arms lifted high that waved a welcome to him. Forty years, and there were signs of adolescence, such as a tree experiences—a noticeable maturity of form with the life-stream still running strong—a dignity, a majesty, becoming, awe-inspiring, overpowering when one thought of its humble beginning. The great, out-stretched rounded top seemed like the vast dome of a cathedral, and the sunshine and shadow of spring and summer and fall that sifted through the branches traced in weird and fanciful imagery the varying moods of the seasons, so that it seemed as though the vast spaces of this sanctuary were spread with colorful tapestries and rugs, rare, ancient, priceless!

Fifty years, and Ralph Parsons from his faraway home in Nebraska, wrote now and then to friends in the near neighborhood of the cottonwood tree, eager for some word of it. And these friends to whom he appealed, knowing his peculiar veneration for the tree, would write in answer, briefly but reassuringly: "It's bigger than ever and going strong!"

Sixty years, and one day Ralph Parsons, bowed of form, slow of step and with hair as white as the virgin snow, appeared at the home of a friend in Aroma Park. Though for him the sands of life were running low and a thousand miles had intervened, he hungered for one last communion with this old cottonwood tree which had figured so prominently in his life and his thoughts that it had become an obsession. There are men still living who accompanied Ralph Parsons to the spot on the Payne farm that memorable morning. Vainly they try to tell you of the mingled expressions of awe and reverence that shone in his thin, pale face, as the rugged lines of this prairie giant loomed before him crowned with all the glory of its summer verdure. Ralph Parsons, a man with the soul of a poet, was a man of peculiar moods as his neighbors knew, and there was a moment of hushed silence, a constraint that became in a way irksome as he walked into the tree's far-flung shadow and doffed his hat as though its precincts were like unto a holy place. Ah, it was indeed a holy place for Ralph Parsons. Here, in the very heart of this living thing, were enshrined memories of his youth, and as he stood there two thin, gaunt arms reached outward and upward towards the massive form of the cottonwood, and tears rained down his rugged cheeks, and for many minutes he stood thus and no word was spoken. It was an awkward moment for the friends who had accompanied Ralph Parsons on this friendly mission but, they remembered, Ralph always was odd in a way. These men have said that no word was spoken but, again, they did not understand. The voice of the Infinite spoke to Ralph Parsons from the high altar of "The Cathedral of the Prairie"—"Peace to thee, friend! Blessed is he who thus reared a temple to the Most High!"

Seventy years, and Ralph Parsons had long been summoned to his reward. He did not long survive his trip. But the cottonwood, with its life-stream still mounting high, waxed in strength and stature so that the afternoon sun, dropping down from the zenith to the west, causes the tree's huge shadow to creep eastward, unfolding like a living thing over the road, down the river bank and far out onto the limpid surface of the Kankakee. Eighty years, and it still stands, a mighty thing nurtured by those mysterious, unseen forces, that dominate the realm of nature. Its top has a sweep of an hundred feet; its primary branches have attained the dimensions of venerable forest trees; its sturdy trunk has a girth of fifteen feet seven inches, and where the main roots reach out to grip mother earth there it has a girth of eighteen feet! There is a virility beneath the rugged exterior that proclaims a destiny unfulfilled by many decades. It is sound to the core! It has neither spot nor blemish! Jove's thunderbolts, as if by some definitely ordered plan, have spared it, lo, these many years, and the fierce winds and storms of summer and winter have wrestled with it in vain. Even the destructive sleet storms have left its symmetry unmarred. It still looms in unwonted majesty and beauty, the most striking land-mark in all the country roundabout, this cottonwood slip which a man rescued on the prairie on an afternoon in the long ago, when the world was new! To all men who view it, it is a living example of the truth as proclaimed by the poet—

"God asks so little, and gives so much When a man plants a tree!"

Books by Kevin McNulty, Sr.

"Around Momence" by Kevin McNulty, Sr.
Copyright © 2007 Kevin McNulty, Sr.
Published by Arcadia Publishing
Charleston SC, Chicago IL, Portsmouth NH, San Francisco, CA
ISBN   978-07358-57289

"Lt. Pat O'Brien" by Kevin McNulty, Sr.
Copyright © 2013 KMC PUBLISHING COMPANY
All rights reserved.
ISBN: 10-0615852114
ISBN-13: 978-0615852119

"The Barns of Kankakee County" by Kevin McNulty, Sr.
Copyright © 2014 KMC PUBLISHING COMPANY
All Photography is the property of Kevin McNulty, Sr.
ISBN-10: 0989796515
ISBN-13: 978-0-9897965-1-4

"Finding Pat O'Brien," by Kevin McNulty, Sr
Copyright © 2014 KMC PUBLISHING COMPANY
All rights reserved.
ISBN-10: 0989796523
ISBN-13: 978-0-9897965-2

"A Kid from Momence…Growing up After the War," by Kevin McNulty, Sr.
Copyright © 2015 KMC PUBLISHING COMPANY
All rights reserved.
ISBN-10:   098979654X
ISBN-13:   978-0-9897965-4-5

"Assessing Music Performance...A Valid System for Measuring Student Performance and Growth"
By Kevin McNulty, Sr
Copyright © 2018 KMC PUBLISHING COMPANY
All rights reserved
ISBN 13 978-0-9897965-8-3

"American Character...Have We Change?"
By Kevin McNulty, Sr.
Copyright @ 2018 KMC PUBLISHING COMPANY
All Rights Reserved
ISBN-13: 978-0-9897965-7-6
ISBN-10: 0-9897965-7-4

Other books published by KMC Publishing Company

"Outwitting the Hun," by Lieutenant Pat O'Brien
Harper W Brothers Publishers
NEW YORK AND LONDON 1918 - PUBLIC DOMAIN 2013
New York and London, 1918, Public Domain

Republished
Copyright (2) 2013 KMC PUBLISHING COMPANY
All Rights Reserved
ISBN - 0989796507
ISBN - 978-0-9897965-0-7

KMC PUBLISHING COMPANY

KMC PUBLISHING COMPANY
P.O. Box 1505
Matteson, IL 60443
Kevin McNulty, Sr. Publisher
www.kmcpublishingcompany.com
kevin@kmcpublishingcompany.com
708-747-9182 (0)
708- 843-9012 (f)

Made in the USA
Monee, IL
08 June 2024

59609919R00142